VAMPIRES, WEREWOLVES & ZOMBIES

VAMPIRES, WEREWOLVES & ZOMBIES

LISA REGAN

tangerine press®

an imprint of

Scholastic

www.scholastic.com

an imprint of
SCHOLASTIC
www.scholastic.com

Scholastic and Tangerine Press and associated logos are trademarks
of Scholastic Inc.

Published by Tangerine Press, an imprint of Scholastic Inc.,
 557 Broadway; New York, NY 10012

Scholastic Canada Ltd.
Markham, Ontario

Scholastic Australia Pty. Ltd
Gosford NSW

Scholastic New Zealand Ltd.
Greenmount, Auckland

Scholastic UK
Coventry, Warwickshire

1 2 3 4 5 6 7 8 9 10

ISBN: 978-0-545-21473-5

Editorial and design by
Amber Books Ltd
Bradley's Close
74–77 White Lion Street
London N1 9PF
United Kingdom
www.amberbooks.co.uk

Project Editor: Sarah Uttridge
Design: Rajdip Sanghera

Printed in China

Picture credits: All illustrations by Mike Taylor and Tom Connell/The Art Agency
© Amber Books Ltd.

Contents

Introduction

Tales of monstrous beings have been told for centuries. Around the world, people swap stories about local characters, strange sightings in nearby areas, and creatures that haunt the night. Sensible people stay in their homes.

These myths or folk tales are part of history's oral tradition. Long before television, computers, or even books, communities passed on spoken stories, from parents and grandparents to sons and daughters. Sometimes these tales are based on facts, but the very nature of oral tradition means that stories are changed, exaggerated, and made scarier each time they are told.

Characters in the stories often have things in common, but may be slightly different from one country to another. In countries where wolves were not feared, people talked about more common creatures as were-beasts: were-jaguars, were-bears, and were-tigers. Classic werewolves change from a human to a wolf whenever there is a full moon, and can be shot with a silver bullet. Yet in some versions, werewolves are afraid of anything made of silver, and can change shape at any time if they have the right kind of magic.

Vampire stories—tales of humans who feed on blood—are relatively new, especially in the Western world. Many can be traced back to early works such as *Carmilla*, *The Vampyre*, and Bram Stoker's *Dracula*. These books use old myths and historical characters, and have inspired twenty-first century creations of popular and up-to-date horror characters on screen and in novels.

Zombies are undead, ghoulish creatures that rise from their graves and haunt the living. They are linked to voodoo rituals. Tales are told in many different cultures, each of them adding their own ethnic twist on how the monsters are created or destroyed.

Bram Stoker's Dracula

AGE
Count Dracula is centuries old, but because of his blood-sucking habits he never ages. After he has feasted he revitalizes; his white hair becomes darker and his skin less pale.

MOUTH
When the Count smiles he reveals his pointed white teeth. He has a cruel mouth with unnaturally red lips.

HEAD
His ears are very pale and pointed at the top, his cheeks are also pale and thin, and he has a mustache and bushy eyebrows that almost meet in the middle. His white hair is thinning at the front but thick everywhere else.

HANDS
Jonathan Harker notices that the Count has hairs growing in the palms of his pale, broad hands. His nails are long and very pointed.

Count Dracula is the main character in Bram Stoker's 1897 book *Dracula*. He is a shape-shifting vampire who can change into various creatures such as a bat or a giant dog, and also into fog, to allow him to move into locked rooms. He holds Jonathan Harker prisoner in Castle Dracula, but keeps him alive for his own purposes. Harker nearly becomes the victim of three female vampires—the Count's wives—but the Count saves him. Dracula casts no reflection in a mirror, and cannot bear sunlight, garlic, or crosses. To kill him, he must be stabbed in the heart with a stake; then he crumbles to dust.

SIZE

▶ ALTHOUGH DRACULA SPARES HARKER'S LIFE, he is not so kind to Harker's fiancée, Mina, and her friend Lucy. Lucy becomes a vampire herself, and has to be killed with a stake through the heart and then beheaded. Mina is bitten by Dracula, and he feeds her with his own blood to form a dangerous bond between them. Only when Dracula dies will Mina be free from this curse. A group of Lucy and Mina's friends track down Dracula, who has fled back to his home in Transylvania, and manage to kill him.

WHERE IN THE WORLD?

The Count lives in Castle Dracula, in the Carpathian Mountains, on the border of Transylvania, Bukovina, and Moldavia.

TRANSYLVANIA

CARPATHIAN MOUNTAINS

DID YOU KNOW?

● When Harker stays at Castle Dracula, he is puzzled by the Count's behavior. He never eats or drinks, and he sleeps all day and works at night. Gradually, Harker begins to realize what sort of creature Dracula really is.

● At times, Harker sees Dracula climb out of a castle window and run down the stone walls just like a lizard, with his large cloak billowing around him.

● Parts of the novel are set in Whitby in Yorkshire, England, where Bram Stoker spent many vacations. In the story, Dracula sails to Whitby, devouring the ship's crew along the way.

● Dracula dies in his coffin, but not with a stake through the heart. He has his throat cut and his heart stabbed with a knife—but is that enough to finish him off forever, or could the Count rise again one day?

Lord Ruthven

PERSONALITY
His awe-inspiring presence is very grim: he silences laughter with a look, and has a supernatural, unworldly appearance.

EYES
Even in the liveliest human company, Lord Ruthven has dead, gray eyes that look at other people like a weight pressing down on them.

FACE
His face is deathly pale. He never blushes or gets more color, even when he is angry.

CLOTHING
To fit in with high-society circles, Lord Ruthven wears fashionable clothes made of fine materials, with a hat, collar, and gloves.

Lord Ruthven is a strange kind of vampire. He remains aloof in society, although women are fatally attracted to him. He has a reputation for hating vice, but in fact is a gambler and supporter of beggars and lowlifes. He keeps his vampire diet well hidden so even his traveling companion, Aubrey, fails to guess how he lives. He appears to be mortally wounded, and Aubrey leaves Greece thinking his friend is dead. But Lord Ruthven cannot be killed so easily, and returns to hunt down Aubrey's nearest and dearest.

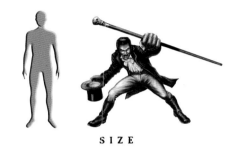

SIZE

▶ NO GOOD EVER COMES to the people who become close to Lord Ruthven. Aubrey suffers as the Greek girl he admires, followed by his beloved sister, both fall prey to the Lord's vampiric appetite. At first, Aubrey is unaware of what Lord Ruthven really is. By the time Aubrey realizes, it is too late. He has given his oath that he will not betray the Lord, and his sister is due to be married to him before his oath can be broken. Aubrey writes her a letter, but she becomes the vampire's victim before she has the chance to read the warning.

WHERE IN THE WORLD?

Lord Ruthven befriends Aubrey in London and they travel together through Europe to Greece, where Ruthven preys upon a peasant girl called Ianthe.

ENGLAND

GREECE

DID YOU KNOW?

● Although Lord Ruthven is a real noble title, and a character of the same name appeared in the 1916 novel *Glenarvon*, the first vampire of this name appeared in John Polidori's 1816 short story, *The Vampyre*.

● Polidori first made up his vampire tale while he was traveling with a circle of writers who challenged each other to invent a horror story. In the same group was Mary Shelley, who came up with the story of *Frankenstein*, which was published in 1818.

● The Greek girl, Ianthe was the daughter of an innkeeper. Aubrey stayed at the inn when in Greece. She tells him local tales of vampires, and the signs they leave on their victims, but he does not believe her.

● Aubrey tries to break his oath and warn his sister about Lord Ruthven. However, he falls ill and doctors think he has mental problems, so his warnings are ignored.

Carmilla

HAIR
Like all rich young women of this period in history, Carmilla has long, flowing locks of hair that swirl around her shoulders and down her back.

BEAUTY
Carmilla captivates her victims with her beauty. She has the blushing, dimpled cheeks of an innocent girl, with a soft, enticing voice and full lips.

VAMPIRE LOOKS
Don't be fooled by those cherubic features—by night they transform into the hot lips and flashing dark eyes of a hungry vampire.

HANDS
Her hands show an extraordinary strength for such a slender girl; she can grip a man's wrist so he cannot move, and her grasp leaves a strange numb feeling that sometimes never fades.

BODY
Carmilla is tall and slim, with a catlike grace even in her human form.

In the 1872 story *Carmilla*, the main character is a vampiress who only chooses girls as her victims. She will often befriend them before starting to feed upon them at night. She tends to sleep during the daytime, ready to stalk the corridors and bedchambers of her prey while they rest. Carmilla herself sleeps in a coffin. She becomes companion to Laura, a lonely 18-year-old who recognizes Carmilla from a dream or vision she had some 12 years before. Little does Laura know, but Carmilla is one of the undead, also known as the Countess Mircalla Karnstein, who has been around since the late 1600s.

SIZE

▶ TO PREY UPON HER VICTIMS, Carmilla assumes the form of a fiendish black cat. She creeps into their bedrooms at night and bites them on the neck or chest. Many of them feel this as if in a dream, and Laura has no wounds as proof that a vampire has visited her. After feeding, Carmilla turns back into a woman and leaves through the closed door, or drifts easily through the solid walls of the room. Her victims usually die after she has drunk from them.

WHERE IN THE WORLD?

Carmilla moves into the castle of Laura and her father, in the Austrian state of Styria.

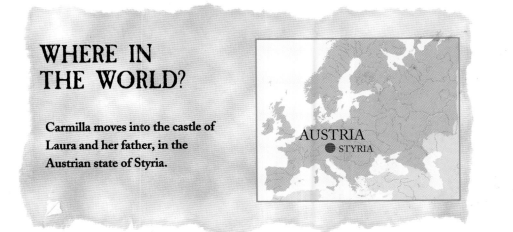

AUSTRIA
● STYRIA

DID YOU KNOW?

● The story was written by Joseph Sheridan le Fanu in 1872. It is thought to have been a major influence on Bram Stoker when he wrote *Dracula* some 25 years later.

● Carmilla takes on different names to befriend different people, and in various periods of history, but they are all anagrams: Carmilla, Mircalla, Millarca.

● With the help of Baron Vordenburg, an authority on vampires, the tomb of Carmilla is tracked down. Her body is exhumed and destroyed so that no more young girls will fall victim to her charms and appetite.

● A vampire named Carmilla has appeared in *Doctor Who*, the anime *Helsing*, various comics and video games, and many different movies. Not bad for the first ever female fictional vampire!

Lestat

HAIR
All of Lestat's kind have long, flowing locks. Lestat's hair is blond and curls below his ears.

EYES
A vampire's eyes are fierce and pale—somehow paler than you would expect from the color of their hair. They can cry, but shed tears only once or twice in their life of eternity.

TEETH
The vampire's teeth give away his true nature. Even in a beautiful face, the teeth are yellowed and pointed— perfect for sucking blood.

NAILS
These vampires have long, pointed nails that look as if they are made of glass.

SKIN
Lestat has skin that heals instantly if it is cut, and he never ages.

Lestat is a rare kind of vampire, one of the "New World" of fiends preying on the people of the southern United States. He has cold skin and eyes like a devil, but is strangely fascinating and attractive to his victims. It is in his nature to kill, and a strange peace washes over him each time he claims another human life. Mostly, his victims feel no pain as he sinks his teeth into their flesh and drains their blood to quench his thirst. He wears a pointed silver thimble on the thumb of his right hand, and sometimes uses this to pierce a victim's skin and drain their blood into a wine glass.

SIZE

▶ LURKING AROUND NEW ORLEANS, Lestat finds a victim named Louis, who has lost the will to live since his wife and child died. Lestat drinks his blood, but gives Louis the choice to join him in eternal life. When Louis accepts, Lestat slits his own wrist and lets his vampire blood flow into Louis' mouth. As Louis drinks, he seals his own fate: he will never grow old or die, and can prey upon people with Lestat for all time. He realizes, though, that few vampires have the stamina for immortality, and that Lestat's lifestyle is not to his taste.

WHERE IN THE WORLD?

Lestat transforms Louis just south of New Orleans, but persuades him to move to the city for more choice of fresh blood.

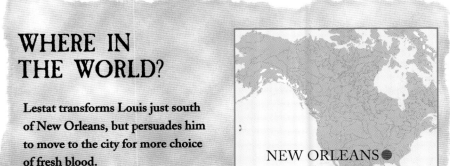

NEW ORLEANS ●

DID YOU KNOW?

● The vampires never grow old, and look the same as when they were first taken away from their human life. Louis meets Armand in Paris: he is the oldest living vampire, and is about 400 years old.

● There are many "Old World" vampires living in Europe. Like Lestat, they have superhuman powers. They can move extremely fast, and some can fly. Many of them have the ability to read each others' thoughts.

● Sunlight will cause great pain and burn a vampire's skin, quickly reducing their body to ashes. Vampires can be burned to death or slashed in half to kill them.

● Lestat appears in *The Vampire Chronicles* written by Anne Rice, and in the movie *Interview with the Vampire*.

Edward Cullen

EYES
His eyes vary in color, from a golden butterscotch shade of topaz to coal-black. The darker they are, the more thirsty he is.

HAIR
Edward's tousled, bronze-colored hair is one of his most striking features and makes him stand out in a crowd.

SKIN
All the vampires in Edward's family are pale-skinned and devastatingly beautiful, but often have dark circles under their eyes.

BODY
Edward is much, much stronger than he looks. He can carry Bella in one hand and has to be careful not to crush her by accident when they embrace.

TEETH
Of course, Edward has the sharp teeth of a vampire, but they aren't usually noticeable. It is only during conflict or feeding that he bares his teeth and lets out a vicious, guttural snarl.

The Cullen family is an unusual breed of modern vampire; they don't drink human blood and prey only upon wild animals. Edward's favorite is the mountain lion, but his brother Emmett prefers grizzly bear. They live a relatively normal life, attending high school or working in the community, but are aloof and other-worldly. They are all very strong, and can move at lightning speed. Both of these skills help in their hunt for a meal. Add to that their venomous bite and their physical attractiveness, it's easy to see how they have survived for centuries.

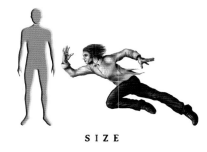

SIZE

▶ EDWARD MEETS BELLA when she moves to live with her father. He is drawn to her, even though he knows it could be fatal for her. He is attracted by her smell; something about her scent appeals to his taste buds. He tries to overcome his feelings as a vampire to allow them to develop their relationship. When they finally allow themselves to be alone together, Edward has to overcome the strong urges he feels as he touches Bella's neck and strokes her skin. But is the real danger from Edward, or from the vampires in his company?

WHERE IN THE WORLD?

Edward and his family live and hunt in the small town of Forks, Washington, where it is often cloudy.

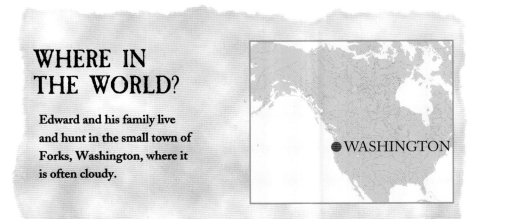

●WASHINGTON

DID YOU KNOW?

● Edward's adoptive father, Carlisle, is a doctor. He works with blood and human bodies every day, but is so settled in his animal-only ways that he is never tempted by the human blood.

● These vampires aren't afraid of the sun, but glitter like diamonds in the sunlight, which means that they stay in the shade to avoid attracting attention.

● All of the vampires have super-heightened senses, but Edward has the additional ability to hear people's thoughts if they are close enough to him.

● There are very few ways to kill these vampires. The best way is to tear him or her to shreds and then burn the pieces.

Eli

SENSES
Eli doesn't feel the cold even in the middle of harsh Swedish winters. She is so sensitive to daylight, however, that she has to cover her windows with cardboard.

GENDER
In the movie, *Let the Right One In*, Eli is a girl, but in the book she starts out as a boy until he is turned into a vampire by the bite of another afflicted person.

SMELL
Eli's friend Oskar notices that Eli sometimes smells bad, depending on how well she has eaten recently.

BLOOD
As a vampire, Eli cannot walk uninvited into a person's home. When Oskar puts this to the test, Eli begins to bleed in patches all over her body.

Eli is a vampire, trying to live an ordinary life in an apartment block in Sweden. Ordinary, that is, except for her guardian Håkan, who has to hunt down victims and drain their blood for Eli to drink. Eli becomes friends with her neighbor, a boy named Oskar. He sees her true nature when she laps up his blood, after he cuts his palm in an offer to become "blood brothers."

SIZE

They remain friends, though, and Eli helps Oskar fight back against bullies. At first, she helps in a human way, but by the end she goes on a killing frenzy, slaughtering three of the people who have been picking on Oskar.

▶ HÅKAN SOMETIMES STRUGGLES to get enough blood to feed Eli. When he can, he gives the victims anesthetic to paralyze them, then hangs them upside down and cuts their throat. He collects the blood in a jug for Eli to drink. However, his first attempts to prey on people in their new home are failures, and Eli starts to feel hungry and weak. Håkan eventually offers her his own blood, straight from his neck; after Eli has drunk her fill, Håkan falls from a tall building and dies, leaving Eli to fend for herself.

WHERE IN THE WORLD?

Eli and Håkan move into the apartment next door to Oskar, in the Swedish town of Stockholm.

●SWEDEN

DID YOU KNOW?

● Eli's victim Virginia is turned into a vampire herself after she is bitten by Eli. Rather than endure this fiendish life, she kills herself. As vampires cannot bear sunlight, she opens the blinds of her room in broad daylight and bursts into flames.

● Among Eli's supernatural, vampiric powers are the ability to climb the outside of buildings, and to flit from window to window, even two stories up.

● Oskar is 12 years old and thinks that Eli is around the same age, but when he asks she can't remember her birth date. It is only when Oskar realizes what she really is that he figures out why Eli doesn't celebrate a birthday.

● Eli and Oskar appear in the movie and novel *Let the Right One In*, by Swedish author John Ajvide Lindqvist.

The Hound of the Baskervilles

MOUTH
The dog has fiery jaws that can be clearly seen even in the gloom of the moors at night. It is said that flames seem to burst from its mouth.

EYES
All of the tales from the *Hound of the Baskervilles* focus on its evil, glowing eyes, which make it look like a dog belonging to the devil.

BODY
The black dog has a huge, powerful body and is the size of a calf.

FEET
Although described as a "hellhound," the dog is certainly not made up or ghostly, as its feet leave large footprints at the scene of one of its attacks.

This fearsome dog is described as "a spectral hound, black, silent and monstrous" and roams the deserted, boggy lands of Dartmoor. Many locals claim to have seen the dog. It lurks near the rocks and caves, and no local person ever considers walking across the moor at night. It is not always so silent: its cries can be heard for miles. The nighttime air throbs with the wild,

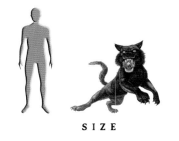

SIZE

menacing howls that pierce the ears and chill the blood of everyone who knows the tale of the fearsome creature. Occasionally, it approaches the houses at the edge of the moor, and more than one person becomes its victim after failing to outrun it.

▶ THE HOUND'S FIRST VICTIM is Sir Charles Baskerville. He is found dead at the end of his own garden, where he was chased by the monstrous canine. The dog was able to leap into the garden over a gate, and the poor man fled from the fiendish-looking creature. The hound's next victim is chased across the moors, where he falls to his death while trying to escape the dog's vicious jaws. The beast attacks a third victim who is on his walk home, the dog jumped out of the chilling fog that often swirls across Dartmoor.

WHERE IN THE WORLD?

The Hound of the Baskervilles roams the moors of Devon in England, and is the curse of the Baskerville family who live near Dartmoor.

DEVON
● DARTMOOR

DID YOU KNOW?

● The hound is a creation of Sir Arthur Conan Doyle in his 1902 Sherlock Holmes story *The Hound of the Baskervilles.*

● Dr. Watson (Holmes' friend and assistant) hears the cry of the hound and describes it as "a long, low moan, indescribably sad, [which] swept over the moor ... From a dull murmur it swept into a deep roar and then sank back into a melancholy, throbbing murmur once again."

● The Baskerville family has been cursed by the hound for centuries. The curse started with the horrific deeds of Sir Hugo Baskerville, a cruel and vicious man who was eventually killed by a ghostly black dog.

● It turns out that the dog is a real one, with luminous paint around its face to give it the appearance of blazing fire.

The Infected (from *I Am Legend*)

SKIN
When seen in daylight, the creatures' skin appears see-through, and their veins are visible. Sunshine burns their flesh and they have to stay in the darkness to survive.

HAIR
The Infected lose all of their hair as a result of the infection.

INFECTION
The virus makes an infected person or dog's gums bleed, their pupils become dilated, and clumps of their hair fall out almost instantly.

SPEECH
The infected beings cannot talk anymore, but they growl and snarl like a pack of animals or monsters.

TEETH
The Infected have rotten, pointed teeth like fangs that they use to attack and eat with.

The Infected are a kind of vampire-zombie. They were created by a powerful manmade virus and are strong, fast, and almost unstoppable. The virus can also be transmitted between dogs, and the zombies are accompanied by hairless canines that help with their hunting. The Infected prowl at night, feeding on wildlife that roam city streets, and searching for the one man who is trying to destroy them: Dr. Neville. He is immune to the virus, but the Infected have enough intelligence to gang together and try to hunt him down.

SIZE

▶ IS DR. ROBERT NEVILLE the last human survivor on Earth? That's what he thinks, but as a scientist he feels he should find a cure for the virus that has taken over and created the monstrous Infected. He can leave his house only in daylight hours, and has to cover his scent with bleach when he returns home to stop the Infected from following and attacking him. His house is fully armored with metal shutters, explosives, and a ring of powerful lights to protect him from undead intruders.

WHERE IN THE WORLD?

Dr. Neville patrols New York City, trying to find a cure for the virus. As far as he knows, the mutants may occupy the entire world, with him as the only human survivor.

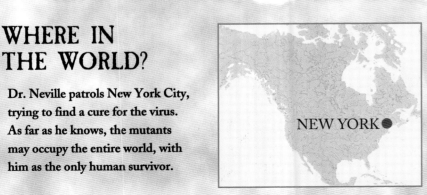

NEW YORK ●

DID YOU KNOW?

● The Infected can be blown up, burned, or killed by gunfire; Robert Neville always keeps a rifle and pistol close at hand. A bullet in the chest is a sure way of wiping out an Infected.

● Will Smith stars in the 2007 movie *I Am Legend*, based on a 1954 book with the same name written by Richard Matheson. Two other movies have been based on the novel: *The Last Man on Earth* and *The Omega Man*.

● The title comes from the fact that vampires used to be the stuff of legend, but now they are the ordinary ones, while Dr. Neville is the legend.

● Matheson's novel was also the inspiration for the movie *Night of the Living Dead*. Both the novel and the movie deal with a heroic man fighting for survival against the evil undead, and trying to save life as he knows it.

Elizabeth Bathory

MIND
Elizabeth's beautiful exterior kept her wicked interior hidden from the world. Few could imagine that a gorgeous-looking woman was capable of such evil acts.

FACE
The Countess was often spoken about because of her beauty, and it was the desire to keep this reputation that made her look for unusual and gruesome beauty products.

CLOTHES
The noble classes from this period of history wore colorful, fine outfits with many layers and ruffles. Their jewels showed others how rich they were.

SKIN
Her skin was pale, clear, and blemish-free, and she was very proud of its youthful appearance.

TEETH
Not as you would expect—these are not the teeth of a vampire. But the tales of her blood-lust suggest that Bram Stoker knew her story when he was writing *Dracula*.

Elizabeth Bathory wasn't the invention of a writer, but a real noblewoman who was born in the sixteenth century. She lived in a castle with her faithful servants who assisted her with her evil crimes: capturing and torturing young girls. It is said that Elizabeth held as many as 600 young women captive, and she is often known as "The Blood Countess." She took great delight in causing pain and humiliating her victims, but her crimes escalated when she began to believe that their blood would help to preserve her youth and beauty. This idea was confirmed by her servants, who were rumored to be witches.

SIZE

▶ As Elizabeth sat in her bedroom having her hair styled, her nervous servant pulled her hair and hurt Elizabeth's head. Elizabeth flew into a rage, and smacked the girl so hard that blood flew, landing upon Elizabeth's hand. She thought that it had an instant effect on her skin, making it look younger. But that wasn't enough for the wicked countess. She began to kill her victims so that she could take a bath in their blood. She may even have drunk their blood like a vampire to feel its full effect.

WHERE IN THE WORLD?

The Countess committed most of her crimes at Castle Cachtice, but moved to Vienna in Austria when she thought she had been found out.

VIENNA
● CASTLE CACHTICE

DID YOU KNOW?

● Born in Hungary, Elizabeth's true name was Báthory Erzsébet. Elizabeth is the English form of the name.

● As a child, Elizabeth may have been mentally ill, leading to her fiendish behavior as an adult. She was used to witnessing cruel acts of punishment: one story describes a thief who was caught and sewn into the belly of a dying horse, with only his head left out, and left like that until he died.

● To start with, the Countess chose servants and peasants as her victims, and carried out her crimes for years without being accused. Her evil deeds could no longer be ignored when she began to attack young noble girls.

● Elizabeth was eventually held prisoner in her own castle. She was walled into her bedchamber, with only slits left for air and food, and died there after about three years.

Lamia

EYES

She is cursed to have her eyes permanently open, but later Zeus grants her the power to pluck out her own eyeballs to relieve her from the torture of images of her lost children.

HEAD

Lamia has a human head with the face of a beautiful young woman. She was so attractive that she tempted Zeus, the most important of the Greek gods, to fall in love with her.

TEETH

With her mouth closed, Lamia is a beautiful temptress. Look inside, though, and you'll see the vicious teeth she needs to devour young children.

BODY

The top half of Lamia's body takes human form. The bottom half is the golden-speckled body of a snake or serpent.

I s Lamia a monster, a woman, a vampire, or a witch? Tales are told that combine all of these. Commonly, she is a demon who roams at night, invading households to drink the blood of children. Sometimes she steals children from their beds. It may be that she was transformed into a half-human, half-serpent by her grief over the death of her children. In some cultures she is linked to Lilith, a night-demon who can appear as an owl, and disturbs people in their sleep. She can bring upsetting dreams and even disease and illness.

SIZE

▶ NEVER FALL IN LOVE WITH somebody who is already married—especially if he is a Greek god with a jealous wife. Zeus may even have had children with Lamia, and his wife Hera was furious and swore revenge. She killed Lamia's children and condemned her to a life with no sleep. Unable to close her eyes, Lamia could never escape the vision of her dead sons and daughters. Her only comfort was to hunt down other people's offspring and take out her torment on them.

WHERE IN THE WORLD?

The great god Zeus ruled from Mount Olympus in ancient Greece, north of Athens. Tales of Lamia are told worldwide to tame disobedient children.

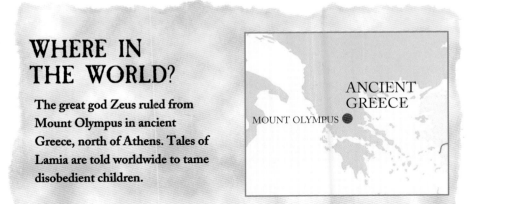

ANCIENT GREECE

MOUNT OLYMPUS ●

DID YOU KNOW?

● Later versions of Lamia describe her as an out-and-out vampire, drinking the blood of any human whether they are children or adults.

● Poets and artists from the Romantic movement of the late eighteenth and early nineteenth centuries depict Lamia as a blood-sucking monster who can take the form of a beautiful woman. She has an ordinary body but is often shown with snakeskin adornments.

● In one story, Lamia is daughter of the sea-god Poseidon, and appears as a shark. In others, where she is portrayed as a beautiful she-demon, she starts life as a Libyan queen.

● Lilith appears in Jewish tales and in the King James version of the Bible. Stories name her as Adam's first wife, before Eve.

Strigoi

HEARTS
Strigoi are often said to have two hearts next to each other.

FACE
A strigoi will show signs of being undead around the face: it may simply be pale and washed out, or more frightening with hollow, red-rimmed eyes and traces of blood from its feeding frenzies.

CLOTHES
If a strigoi has risen from the grave, this is often apparent by the decayed state of its clothing.

HANDS
Bony, skeletal hands and dirty, broken fingernails are telltale signs that the strigoi has been buried underground.

ANIMAL FORM
Some strigoi steal the form of an animal—usually a cat, dog, or sheep—and can transform themselves into this shape to leave their own body at night.

The strigoi is an evil force that is difficult to get rid of. The strigoi are usually troubled souls that rise from the grave to seek justice for something wrong done to them during their lifetime. They are thirsty for blood, and can spend many nights hunting for food. They have to return to their grave regularly until they become older and stronger, when they need only return to it every Saturday. If a strigoi is not destroyed after seven years, it no longer has to return to its grave but can move to live wherever it likes, looking like any normal person.

SIZE

▶ AFTER RISING FROM THEIR GRAVE, the strigoi pass through different stages. In its first stage it is like a poltergeist, moving furniture and causing trouble in its old home. At this stage it is invisible, and often steals human food to eat. After this, it returns to the form it had when alive: visible although sometimes the worse for wear after being buried. It feeds on livestock until it is strong enough to become a true undead creature. Even then, it still torments its family, choosing family members as its first victims to feed on their blood.

WHERE IN THE WORLD?

The strigoi are famous in Romanian mythology; the area of Transylvania, famous in many vampire stories, is in Romania.

TRANSYLVANIA ●

ROMANIA

DID YOU KNOW?

● Sometimes strigoi are known as moroi, most often in the countryside.

● Strigoi can be tricked into leaving their victims alone by scattering seeds with a nail hidden within. The obsessive creatures cannot pass without counting the seeds; the hidden nail will prick them and force them to start counting all over again.

● Some types of strigoi can leave their body in the form of a spark of light that can zoom through the air.

● Most strigoi drink blood directly from their victim's heart. Their own hearts (although they have two) are their vulnerable spot: they can be killed by driving a stake through them.

● It used to be thought that an unmarried person would return from death as a strigoi, and prey upon their former lovers. They must be killed with a sickle through the heart.

Baobhan Sith

FACE
The women commonly have green eyes and very pale skin and lips. They are unusually beautiful.

HAIR
Often blonde or ghostly white, their hair flows past their shoulders and helps to make them attractive.

CLOTHES
These evil creatures are most often seen wearing a long, green dress and a flowing cloak. Their garments often smell of blood.

FEET
The long robes hide their unusual feet, which take the form of the hooves of a deer.

NAILS
These vampiric ghosts don't have pointed teeth to suck blood: they pierce skin with supremely pointed fingernails and drink from the wounds.

Pronounced "baavan shee," baobhan sith are ghostly vampire-women, who are thought to be related to the banshees of other Celtic myths. They usually gather in forests and wooded areas, and often hang out in groups. Taking the form of beautiful women, they entice men to dance with them. Some tales say that they have hypnotic powers to help them do this. When the

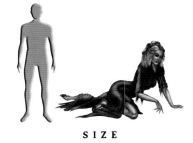

SIZE

men are captivated by their dance, and usually too exhausted or entranced to fight back, the women pounce on them and feast on their blood. The victims are sucked dry, and left for dead. A baobhan sith's feared substance is iron.

▶ FOUR MEN were traveling through the forest, and stopped for the night in a clearing. They played music and danced, and one of the men wished that he had a female partner to dance with. Four beautiful women suddenly appeared. Three of them danced with the travelers, while the fourth stood with the musician. It was this man who noticed blood streaming from his friends. He ran and hid in their circle of horses; it was their iron horseshoes that protected him from the baobhan sith until morning.

WHERE IN THE WORLD?

These delicate, dancing fiends are also known as the White Women of the Scottish Highlands.

● SCOTTISH HIGHLANDS

DID YOU KNOW?

● The baobhan sith are often associated with another female demon, the succubus: a woman who seduces men in their sleep.

● Some stories say that the baobhan sith cannot bear sunlight, like many other types of vampire.

● It may be that tales of these evil beings were spread by human women to prevent their husbands from cheating on them.

● Baobhan sith usually prey on hunters who are away from home for a few days, or unsuspecting men who don't get home before darkness falls.

● The Japanese manga series *Helsing* features baobhan sith, as do the fantasy books written by Mark Chadbourn.

Vlad Dracul

FACE
His face betrayed little of his nature: he was stern and wore a mustache, but might only strike fear into the hearts of those who had heard of his reputation.

AGE
Vlad was born in 1431 and died in 1476, when he was 45 years old.

HAIR
Vlad had extremely long, dark hair that billowed behind him when he rode his horse into battle.

CLOTHING
Vlad was a prince and therefore wore fine clothes in keeping with the Romanian fashions of the 1400s.

A real prince from the fifteenth century, Vlad III was the son of "Vlad the Dragon," called Vlad Dracul in his own language. Vlad III thus gained the surname "Draculea," or "Son of Dragon." He is most famous as being the inspiration for Bram Stoker's title character in the 1897 novel *Dracula*. However, Vlad was not a vampire, merely a determined and fierce warrior. His favorite method of torturing and killing his enemies was impaling them on a stake, earning him the nickname Vlad the Impaler. He was Prince of Wallachia, an area in the south of Romania, but lived in Transylvania, with its rich history of vampires.

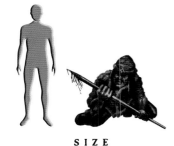

SIZE

▶ VLAD WAS CERTAINLY a heartless man where his enemies were concerned. He killed many thousands of people during his attempts to defend his country against invasion by the Ottoman Empire. One army, on the march toward Wallachia, was stopped in its tracks by a mass of stakes with bodies impaled on them. It is thought that 20,000 Turkish prisoners were put on display to warn off any other would-be attackers. Vlad is also said to have burned and boiled people, and had their hats nailed to their heads.

WHERE IN THE WORLD?

Vlad the Impaler lived in Transylvania but was the ruler of Wallachia, and fought against Hungarians and Turks from the Ottoman Empire.

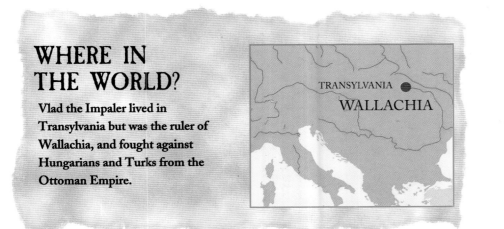

TRANSYLVANIA ●

WALLACHIA

DID YOU KNOW?

● Although he was known for his exceedingly cruel punishments, Vlad is mostly seen by the Romanians as a national savior. His methods were questionable, but he was loyal (and successfully) defended their country.

● It is thought that Bram Stoker read Vlad's name when he was researching Transylvania for vampire folklore. The cruel, bloody character fits the bill (although Vlad's love of stakes wasn't shared by vampires!).

● Vlad's Romanian name is Vlad (short for Vladislav) Tepes.

● Vlad was killed in battle; his head was chopped off and sent to the Turkish Sultan as proof that Vlad the Impaler was actually dead. The Sultan had it put on a stake, in a rather fitting end for a man of Vlad's habits.

Vrykolakes

LIGHT-SENSITIVITY
Unlike many vampires, vrykolakes can roam in daylight hours without coming to harm, although they are most active at night.

WEIGHT
The bodies look bloated and even fatter than when they were alive, which is said to be a result of drinking their fill of blood.

FACE
Despite having been buried underground for some years, the face still has a redness to its complexion.

BODY
You would expect a body to decay once it is buried, but the vrykolakes do not show signs of deterioration.

A vrykolakas (plural vrykolakes) is a dead person who has become a vampire. For much of Greek history, burial sites were hard to find because the islands are so small. Three years after death, bodies had to be dug up so the bones could be removed and the ground used again. If a grave was opened and the body had not decayed, it was believed to be a vrykolakas. This can happen for religious reasons (being excommunicated, living an unholy life, or being buried in unconsecrated ground), but eating meat from a sheep that has been wounded by a werewolf may also turn you into a vrykolakas.

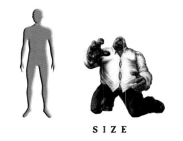

SIZE

▶ A VILLAGE ON THE ISLAND of Crete lived in fear of a vrykolakas. They knew which graveyard it came from, but not which grave. One night, a shepherd took shelter in the graveyard. As he placed his guns by his side to rest, they formed a cross. When the vampire tried to get past that night, the cross stopped him. He and the shepherd argued, and the next day the brave shepherd showed the villagers which grave held the evil creature. It was dug up and a priest was brought to make the undead body holy again.

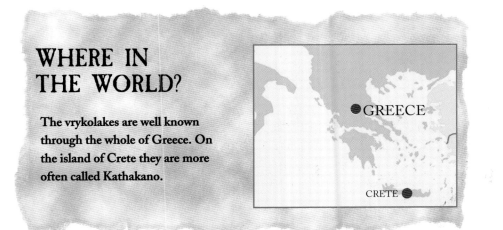

WHERE IN THE WORLD?

The vrykolakes are well known through the whole of Greece. On the island of Crete they are more often called Kathakano.

GREECE

CRETE

DID YOU KNOW?

● A person can become a vrykolakas if a cat jumps over his dead body before it is buried.

● The name vrykolakas is sometimes used specifically for shepherds who have turned into vampires and feed on people and sheep when the moon is full.

● It is said that vrykolakes cannot cross seawater, so any that are captured are reburied on a deserted island to keep the human race safe.

● The creatures can be found and destroyed by a Sabbatarian (someone born on a Saturday, which gives them special holy powers) and their Fetch Dog. If you see a dog on its own, be kind to it, as Sabbatarians can become invisible, so may be watching over their precious dog without you knowing.

Volkodlac

SKIN
The veins can be seen near the surface of a volkodlac's skin, where patches of his tangled fur have fallen out.

EYES
A volkodlac's eyes glow in the dark and have heavy eyebrows that give him a permanently evil look. His pale blue eyes look evil even in his human form, but are terrifying in his wolf's face.

JAWS
His muzzle is pointed like a wolf's, with a mouth full of large, vicious, vampirish teeth.

CLOTHING
Look out for a wolfskin loincloth, or an extra layer of wolfskin worn on the creature's head.

BODY
A volkodlac has the body of a wolfman: he usually walks upright but can prowl on all fours. He has the well-defined torso of a body builder.

In Slavic folktales, the volkodlac spend the daytime in human form and change into wolf form during the hours of darkness. If the werewolf is killed, it becomes a vampire. Once this happens, it can become a werewolf occasionally to satisfy its appetite for flesh and blood. If the vampire is killed and proper precautions are not taken, the cycle starts again and the creature is reborn as a werewolf. It is possible to become a volkodlac by being bitten by one, but this is rare as the monsters usually eat their victims. They feed on animals as well as people.

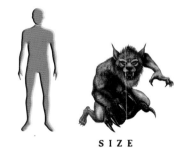

SIZE

▶ DURING THE HARSH EUROPEAN WINTERS, the volkodlacs gather together in groups, mostly in forests. They remove their wolfskins and hang them from the trees. They might decide to release one of their kind from his curse by taking his skin and burning it. The others gather around the fire and dance and howl. This allows the chosen volkodlac to die peacefully and remain at rest. It isn't the kind of gathering you would want to accidentally gatecrash.

WHERE IN THE WORLD?

Most tales of the volkodlacs' wickedness are told by the Slavic people of eastern Europe.

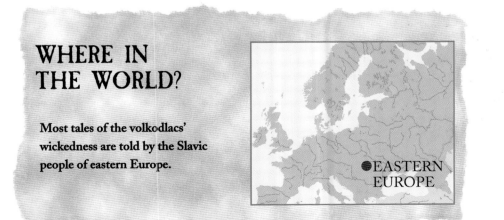

●EASTERN EUROPE

DID YOU KNOW?

● This monster's name appears with many different spellings, such as vlklodak and vulkodlak, depending on which country you are in. The name translates as "wolf's hair."

● If you manage to kill this almost-indestructible beast, you should place a coin in its mouth to stop it from coming back to life in vampire form.

● A human with enough evil in his soul can put on a wolfskin and transform into a volkodlac. When he takes it off, he becomes human again. A person can also drink rainwater taken from the footprint of a wolf.

● Several Slavic stories describe how the creature can be killed by piercing its heart with a pointed stick from an aspen tree.

The Beast of Gévaudan

SIZE
The beast is big—larger than an ordinary wolf. On all fours, it stands as tall as a young cow.

FUR
Although different accounts describe the beast in different colors, it is generally thought that it is reddish-brown, with a gray or white chest.

TAIL
The beast's tail is extremely long and heavy, capable of knocking over or wounding a human adult.

HEAD
The long muzzle contains many huge, pointed teeth. Its ears are small and lie flat on its head.

CLAWS
There are said to be six claws on each of the beast's feet, unlike the four claws of a wolf or the five clawed fingers of some werewolves.

LEGS
With longer back legs, the beast prowls and pounces like a cat, but can walk on its two hind legs like a human. It has been seen wading upright across streams, and attacking on two legs as well.

The beast of Gévaudan, or *la bête du Gévaudan* as it is known in France, was a wolflike creature that preferred the taste of humans to the meat of sheep and cattle. It would walk past a field of cows to attack people (usually children and women) in villages and forests. Some think the creature was really a hyena, a lion, a bear, or a panther. Many thought it was a werewolf. They told tales of a sorcerer who could take the form of a giant wolf that crushed its victims' heads, drank their blood, and ate their flesh.

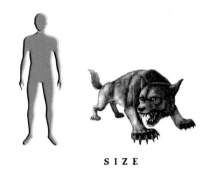

SIZE

▶ AS THE BEAST ROAMED THE COUNTRYSIDE, killing and eating its victims, the villagers decided to hunt it down. They armed themselves with pitchforks and knives, but only managed to scare away the beast. The deaths continued, so King Louis XV sent his troops to track down the monster. Two of them dressed up as women to act as bait. They saw the beast several times, and fired at it, but it always got away. Eventually, a group of men shot the beast with a silver bullet, and the attacks on villages finally stopped.

WHERE IN THE WORLD?

All of the beast's killings took place in the 1760s in Gévaudan in southern France. The area is now part of the département de la Lozère.

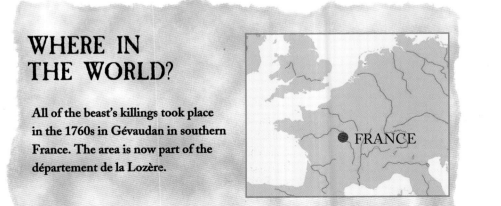

● FRANCE

DID YOU KNOW?

● After its death, the beast's stomach was cut open. Many human bones were found inside.

● The beast's first attack at Gévaudan was near a forest, where it charged at a woman but was fought off by her herd of cattle and bulls with their horns. A month later it returned and killed a teenage girl.

● Some of the beast's victims were found with their clothes carefully removed and laid over their ravaged bodies.

● At times, the beast approached people who were on their way to church, leading to stories that the creature was the devil attempting to stop people from worshipping God.

Werebears

PAWS
One blow from this monster's massive paws is enough to knock its victims unconscious. Its claws are long and vicious enough to kill a full-grown man.

ARMOR
As many werebear tales come from Norse mythology, these creatures are quite often armed with an ax, or may wear body armor.

EYES
A creature of the night, the werebear has glowing eyes that can sometimes be seen from the shadows as it hides, ready to pounce.

BODY
Just as a bear is one of the most powerful mammals, a werebear is extremely strong, with huge muscles and a mighty body.

The werebear is related to the werewolf, but is even more fearsome. Many countries that were home to bears also had folktales of werebears. They were strong and powerful, with signs of human intelligence, and sometimes the skills to use weapons. In Norse history, the Berserkers were a group of warriors who wore bearskins and fought so wildly that they were thought to be werebears. Like werewolves, werebears only transform at certain times, usually linked to the phases of the moon. They often show signs of extreme tiredness once they return to their human state.

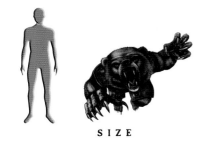

SIZE

▶ A WEREBEAR WILL OFTEN ACT in a bearlike way even in its human form. In one Native American story, a man called Red-breasted Turtle returned from his day's hunting with a deer to feed his family. Four times he killed a deer but was robbed of it on his way home. The man who stole the deer acted strangely, so Red-breasted Turtle lay in wait to see who he really was. He jumped out and killed the strange man by chopping his head off. As the man died, he transformed into a bear.

WHERE IN THE WORLD?

Tales of werebears are told where bears are more feared in the wild than wolves: notably North America, Russia, and parts of Europe.

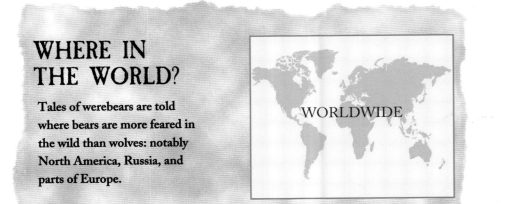

WORLDWIDE

DID YOU KNOW?

● Werebears are strong and fierce and extremely difficult to destroy. If one is killed, it must be burned, together with all the affected person's belongings, to stop it from coming back to life.

● A dead werebear's bones, once burned, should be ground into powder. This powder may be used by a holy man as a cure for the werebear's victims. It can even bring the victims back to life.

● The Berserkers got their name from the bear furs (serks) that they wore. The modern word "berserk" means furious to the point of recklessness, or showing no fear.

Jé-Rouges

EYEBROWS
In their human form, they have thick eyebrows that meet in the middle. The eyebrows remain noticeable and bushy even when in werewolf form.

EYES
The most noticeable feature of this werewolf is its eyes, which glow red in the dark.

TEETH
The massive jaws contain huge, pointed teeth that sink easily into human flesh. Their breath smells of meat and blood.

CLAWS
Like a real wolf, the Jé-rouges has a fifth claw at the back of its leg, a little way above the heel.

The Jé-rouges is a werewolf spirit from the Caribbean nation of Haiti. They are created when a human gives himself over to evil forces or Voodoo leaders in return for being able to change form. It is said that they can change into anything, either plant or animal. The Jé-rouges werewolf chooses the body of an unsuspecting person and possesses them each night. They transform into a cannibalistic wolflike creature that must feed on flesh. Unlike many werewolf myths and legends, the Haitians believe that the Jé-rouges is quite vampirelike, and enjoys biting people to transform them into more of its own kind.

SIZE

▶ THESE CREATURES ARE NOT STUPID—in fact, they are notoriously cunning. One of their favorite tricks is to wake a mother from her sleep. The werewolf asks her, in her groggy state, whether they have her permission to take her child. Of course, the mother is not really awake enough to know what is happening, and is as likely to say yes as she is to refuse and hurry to protect her children as they sleep. If she says yes, Jé-rouges may take the life or just the soul of her child.

WHERE IN THE WORLD?

Tales of Jé-rouges are told throughout the French-speaking country of Haiti, which is on the island of Hispaniola in the Caribbean.

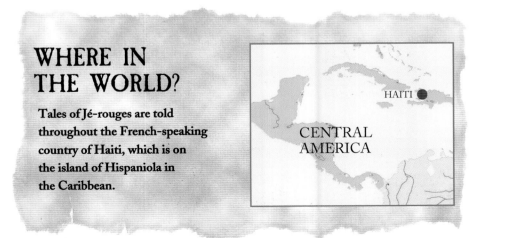

HAITI ●

CENTRAL AMERICA

DID YOU KNOW?

- This creature's name comes from a distortion of the French for red eyes: "*les yeux rouges*." "*Les yeux*" is pronounced "lay jer."

- It is said that the monster will turn back into its human form if you throw an iron, steel hoop, or chain over its head while it is transformed into a wolf.

- Many Haitian people believe in werewolves and warn their children against them. They tell tales of transformed creatures who drive around the neighborhood at dusk, looking for unlucky children to pounce on.

- At birthday parties in Haiti, the children try to take the piece of cake farthest from them. This superstition is supposed to stop them from being turned into a Jé-rouges.

Chupacabra

EYES
The eyes are large and mean. They are usually reported as being black or bright red.

MOUTH
The chupacabra's mouth looks like a small slit that fails to cover the fangs sticking out from its upper and lower jaws.

SKIN
Usually described as gray in color, the chupacabra may have scaly, reptilian skin or mangy, patchy fur. It has spines down its back.

HANDS
Both hands have three fingers and a thumb with strong claws at the end of each one.

COLOR
It's said that the chupacabra can change color like a chameleon. It may look green when seen in sunny clearings or dark brown in the middle of a forest.

MOVEMENT
Reports vary about how the chupacabra gets around. Most agree that it moves on two feet. Some say it jumps like a kangaroo—up to 20 feet (6 m) in a single leap; others even claim it can fly.

The name chupacabra means "goat sucker" and this vampiric creature has a particular liking for goats. Its victims include livestock and pets. Its prey is usually found completely drained of blood. Two or three puncture marks are the telltale sign of the chupacabra: whether these are made with its two largest fangs, or its three claws, no one is sure. The holes are perfectly round and sometimes large enough to insert a human finger. Sometimes, the unfortunate animal has its internal organs mutilated or eaten, with no obvious wounds where the organs could have been removed.

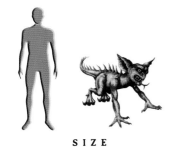

SIZE

▶ ORGANIZED GROUPS OF CHUPACABRA HUNTERS sometimes gather to track down the creature and prevent the mutilation of their livestock. It is believed that the chupacabras live in caves, and some farmers find the cave entrances and start fires to burn the creatures out. Farmers have shot the creature attacking their animals, but these have turned out to be wild dogs and coyotes. Chupacabras' pronounced backbones, and unusually long teeth and claws make them look more like an alien creature than the canines they are.

WHERE IN THE WORLD?

Originally reported in Puerto Rico, there have been chupacabra attacks from the USA down to Brazil and Chile.

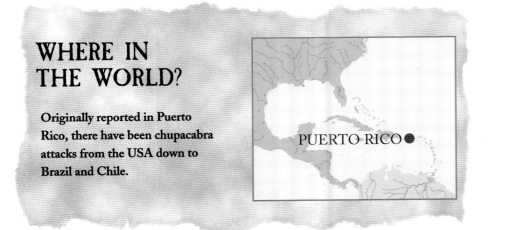

PUERTO RICO ●

DID YOU KNOW?

● According to legend, the chupacabra has a forked tongue and leaves behind a strong smell of sulfur, making people feel sick.

● One theory suggests that the chupacabras are aliens, because of their large oval heads and huge eyes. Some say the creatures are the result of a scientific cross-breeding between animals and aliens.

● The chupacabra is the main creature in the Scooby Doo movie *The Monster of Mexico*.

● Puerto Rico already had its own vampire: El Vampiro de Moco, which worked in a similar way to the chupacabra. This vampire also drained its victims of blood. Eventually it was suggested that these vampires were actually crocodiles that had been illegally released.

Mandurugo

WINGS
To get around, the mandurugo has a pair of wings attached to its body.

FACE
During the daytime, the mandurugo is a beautiful woman. Her features become twisted and evil when she flies out at night looking for food.

EYES
The eyes are bloodshot as a result of staying up all night in search of its prey.

BODY
A mandurugo can detach the top half of its body from its bottom half, which it leaves standing and must return to by morning.

TONGUE
It uses a long, hollow tongue like a butterfly's proboscis to suck the blood from its victims.

There are many tales of vampires told in the Philippines, but most have the same common features. The mandurugo is a beautiful female with a taste for blood. She can detach the upper half of her body from her legs, and grow wings at night to fly off in search of her next victim. She makes a strange "wak-wak" or "tik-tik" noise that is louder the farther away she is. As the sound becomes quieter, it confuses her victims into thinking she is moving away, when actually she is getting closer. She lands on the thatched roof of a house while the people are sleeping. She pokes the victim's skin with her tongue to drink his or her blood.

SIZE

▶ ON ONE ISLAND LIVED a very beautiful woman. She married, but within a year her husband withered away and died. She took another husband, and he died in the same manner. Her third husband also died after just one year. She took a fourth husband, but he was wise to her true nature. He pretended to be asleep, but when he felt something pricking his neck, he took a knife and stabbed the thing on top of him. He heard it fly away into the night. The next day his wife was found dead from a stab wound.

WHERE IN THE WORLD?

The Philippines are made up of many islands, and most of them have their own variation of the mandurugo horror story.

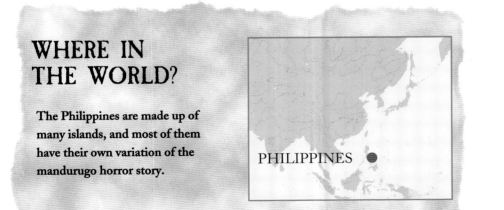

PHILIPPINES ●

DID YOU KNOW?

● These creatures are also called wak-waks, tik-tiks (because of the noise they make), aswangs, or manananggals, depending on which island the tales are told.

● The word "mandurugo" means "bloodsucker." "Manananggal" translates as "separated one."

● Variations in the folklore say that these creatures may have a black chick in their throat, which gives them their evil power, or that they are accompanied by wicked night birds that lead them to the home of their next victim.

● If you can prevent the creature from returning to its bottom half, it will die. You can sprinkle salt on the severed legs, or swap the legs to confuse the top halves.

Jiang Shi

ARMS
Like all dead bodies, jiang shi suffer from rigor mortis (the stiffening of a body after death). This makes them walk with their arms stretched out in front of them.

FINGERNAILS
The fingernails are black, long, and razor sharp. This could be the result of being dead for a long time, or from being buried underground.

CLOTHING
It can take a long time for a body to become a jiang shi, and so their clothes are usually very old-fashioned.

LEGS
Their legs are set solid after death, which makes walking difficult. Instead, jiang shi move with a stiff, strange, jumping motion.

The name "jiang shi" comes from the Chinese for "stiff corpse." Like zombies, jiang shi are dead bodies that can move and hunt down humans. These creatures search for blood and have an endless hunger for it. They also murder people and feed on their life essence as it seeps out. Jiang shi are brain-dead and cannot think, see, or speak, but they seek out their prey either with their sense of smell or by detecting their breathing. It is said that holding your breath might make the difference between capture and escape if you are confronted by one of these monsters.

SIZE

▶ TALES OF JIANG SHI originate from the Chinese custom of transporting dead people back to their hometown to be buried. Priests were paid to carry them and often brought back several corpses at a time, lined up on bamboo rods, which made them look to hop along by themselves. A true jiang shi is only created if the person was particularly wicked while alive, or if they had an improper death such as suicide.

WHERE IN THE WORLD?

Jiang shi are said to travel singly or in groups across China, sometimes covering hundreds of miles to return to their hometown.

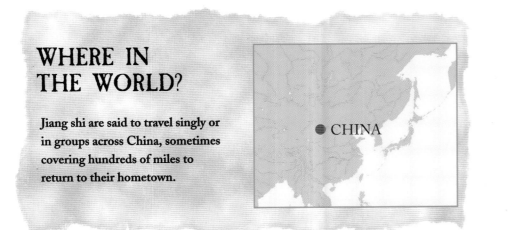

● CHINA

DID YOU KNOW?

● To ward off a jiang shi, you need to write a special spell on thin yellow paper, using chicken's blood as ink, and stick it to its forehead.

● It is also said that rice will stop jiang shi in their tracks. They cannot pass by without stopping to count every single grain. Sticky rice can be used to draw out their evil spirit.

● Jiang shi can be gathered together by an evil master and used as an army of the walking dead. They are sometimes put to work as bodyguards, or can be sent into battle against an enemy.

● Sometimes, jiang shi keep decaying, continuing to look more and more decomposed and terrifying.

Penanggalan

ODOR
Even in human form, the penanggalan smells of vinegar, as she uses so much of it to preserve her decapitated body and to soak her entrails.

HAIR
She grows her hair long, adding to the effect of looking like an octopus when she moves.

FANGS
The penanggalan all have vicious fangs. Many tales say they also have a very long, invisible tongue, which they use to suck blood.

The penanggalan is a Malaysian vampire who is instantly recognizable. By day, she looks like a normal woman—usually a beautiful one, having used witchcraft to enhance her looks. By night, she leaves her body behind, and flies around houses as only a head. She is in search of human blood to drink, and sometimes flesh to eat. She prefers the blood of newborn children or pregnant women, and hangs around screeching while a child is born. She sucks blood with her long, invisible tongue poking into the house. Her victims are not killed instantly but die slowly from disease.

SIZE

▶ ONE DAY, A WOMAN WAS BATHING in a large wooden vat of vinegar. This may have been as a penance, or she may have been meditating, but whatever the reason, she was so caught up in her thoughts that she did not hear a man approach. When he asked the woman what she was doing, she was startled out of her trance. She moved her head up to look at him so quickly that it was ripped off from her body, and the head flew away to a nearby tree.

WHERE IN THE WORLD?

The penanggalan does her wicked work around the Malay Peninsula, a hot area where the houses are commonly built on stilts, allowing her access through the floorboards.

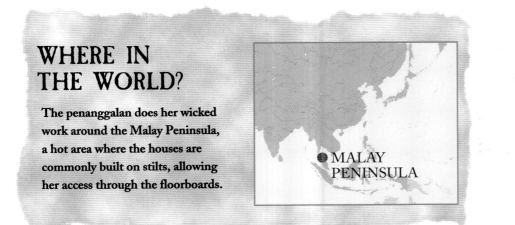

● MALAY PENINSULA

DID YOU KNOW?

● A penanggalan's entrails are said to glow at night, like fireflies.

● Many stories say that the creatures are women who have died in childbirth, or midwives who are in league with the devil.

● To stop a penanggalan from entering your house, you must plant a special thorny plant to grow around the windows and doors. You can also grow spiky pineapples in the space between the ground and the house, which is on stilts, to stop her from coming up through the floorboards.

● While flying at night, the creature's body is left in a vat of vinegar to preserve it. One of the best ways to destroy it is to place glass in the neck, to slash the entrails as they return to their body. They are also vulnerable to ash or crushed garlic if placed in the body.

Asanbosam

TAIL
Some stories say that the vampire has a long tail that ends in the head of a snake. It coils its tail around the branches of trees.

TEETH
This demonic creature is notable for its teeth, which look like human teeth but are made of iron, and deliver a powerful bite.

FEET
The Asanbosam does not have normal feet, but has hooks where its feet should be. It dangles these from trees to capture its prey.

LEGS
Many descriptions of this vampire say it has extremely long legs: long enough to sit in the treetops and still reach its victims on the forest floor.

The Asanbosam is a vampire creature from West African folktales. The Ashanti people of southern Ghana are very afraid of the Asanbosam. It takes a human form, apart from its grisly teeth and hooked legs, but feasts on the blood of people. It will hide in a tree and wait for a passer-by to walk beneath, then hook and bite him on the thumb or big toe to drink his blood. After drinking its fill, the Asanbosam eats the victim's flesh. Sometimes, it plays with the victim for sport, in the way that a cat might play with a mouse.

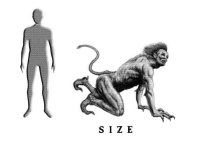

S I Z E

► NOT ALL TREE-DWELLERS with hooked feet are Asanbosam. Watch out for the Naglopers—shape-changers who can adapt their legs to mimic the hooks of the Asanbosam. Naglopers torture the victims they catch. Sometimes they transform their victims into the same shape, and force them to act out the Asanbosam legend. The Naglopers will only restore their victims to their proper shape if they do as they are told and capture innocent people with their hooked feet.

WHERE IN THE WORLD?

Asanbosam tales are most often told in southern Ghana, but the creature is also known in the neighboring countries of Togo and the Ivory Coast.

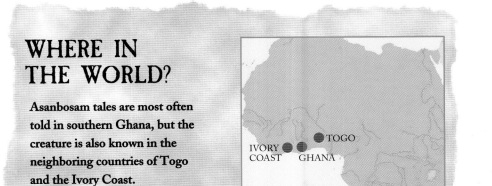

TOGO
IVORY
COAST   GHANA

DID YOU KNOW?

● The creature's name can be spelled in different ways: Asasabonsam and Asanbosam are two of them. However, it is a different sort of monster from Sasabonsam, which has horns and wings.

● According to some tales, the Asanbosam looks human enough to pass as a person in poor light—although its feet are always a giveaway!

● These creatures are so feared that Ghanaian people are reluctant to talk about them. They are seen as an unholy creature, in league with the devil, and can bring bad luck to anyone who speaks their name.

● Many of these tales are told by hunters, as a warning to young boys who are learning to trap and catch their food. It is dangerous to travel in the forests alone, and the Asanbosam tale might teach them to be cautious.

Nocnitsa

FACE
Hidden in shadow, it is hard to see her face, except for her fangs, and the two dots of light that make up her eyes.

HEIGHT
Nocnitsa isn't tall, and looks even shorter because she is hunched over, applying all of her weight to her victim's chest.

LIGHT
Appearing only at night, Nocnitsa seems to consist of flickering shadows, and her lower body trails away into wisps of darkness.

HANDS
Old and gnarled, her hands are crippled with age, and she has vicious talons instead of nails.

Like other nightmarish visions from different parts of the globe, the Nocnitsa creeps into the bedrooms of dreaming people. She sits on their chests and their dreams are filled with the feeling of being pinned down so they cannot move from their own bed. She is also known as the night hag. She preys on children, so it is quite easy for her to keep them still with her body weight, even though she is small. Nocnitsa has a distinct smell of wet moss, soil, and fir trees. This may invade her victim's dreams or linger in the bedroom the morning after her visit.

SIZE

▶ NOCNITSA IS PARTICULARLY frightening for parents with young children. They believe that their precious ones might wake screaming from their nightmares—or worse, never wake up at all. To protect them, they draw a circle around their crib with the point of a knife. Some even leave the knife under the mattress, as it is thought that the metal protects the child. It is also claimed that placing a protective doll or an ax under the floorboards beneath the crib can keep Nocnitsa away.

WHERE IN THE WORLD?

Nocnitsa tales are common in Eastern Europe, including Poland, Russia, and Bulgaria.

RUSSIA ●

● POLAND

● BULGARIA

DID YOU KNOW?

● If you find a stone with a hole in it, keep it as protection from Nocnitsa. It can be hung by your bed at night, and worn around your neck in the daytime.

● In Bulgaria, Nocnitsa is known as Gorska Makua. In Poland she is Krisky or Plaksy. Whatever her name, no good ever comes from her visits, and children are warned to go to sleep quickly and quietly, without fuss and tantrums, so they stay safe and have sweet dreams.

● No one has ever heard her speak, but she can screech and yowl if she is threatened.

● It is not known where Nocnitsa goes in the daytime. She may hide in the forests, or have a concealed home—or she may simply disappear when the Sun rises.

Mara

WINGS
Not everyone agrees whether mara has wings or not—after all, her victims are always sleeping.

BODY
Although weighty enough to trap her victims, in appearance the mara seems light, floaty, and almost see-through.

MOUTH
A nightmarish vision, the mara has an ordinary mouth filled with vicious fangs.

FINGERS
She has long, slender fingers that she entwines in the manes of horses and even the branches of trees.

In Scandinavia, the local version of the night hag is called the mara. She is a spirit being, who seems immaterial until she sits on the chests of her sleeping victims, when she can weigh them down so they are unable to move. The mara can seep into a bedroom through a keyhole or a crack underneath the door. Like the boo hag, she is said to "ride" her victims, but she feeds on their blood while she is riding. It is said that the spirit of any sleeping woman can slip out into the night and become a mara, if the woman is cursed or simply wicked enough.

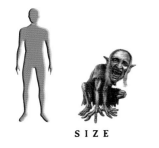

SIZE

▶ A MARA DOES NOT NECESSARILY need human blood to feed upon. She is also partial to the blood of horses. She grabs on to their manes, leaving them tangled and knotted the next morning as evidence that she has been there. These twisted knots are known as "marelocks." The poor horses are left exhausted, frightened, and bathed in sweat when their owners find them. It is also said that a tree with extremely tangled branches is a sign that a mara is roaming the area.

WHERE IN THE WORLD?

The mara works her wickedness in Scandinavia, but she is also known to be seen and felt by sleeping people in other parts of western Europe.

SCANDINAVIA

DID YOU KNOW?

● The word "nightmare" comes from "mara," as the sleeping person usually feels her presence in the form of tormented dreams that are difficult to wake up from.

● Other countries also get their word for nightmare from this hag: nachtmerrie (Netherlands), mareridt (Denmark), cauchemar (France), mardraum or mareritt (Norway), martrö (Iceland), and mardröm (Sweden).

● A woman suspected of being a mara can often be cured by confronting her and saying, "You are a mara" three times over before she runs away.

● In Denmark the name mara is used for all female vampires. In some other countries, the mara has no fangs, but frightens her victims and feeds off their fear.

Banshee

HAIR
A banshee's long hair flows down her back. Often gray or a dull brown in color, it is ragged and knotted.

EYES
Look out for a banshee's eyes! They are red from crying, and usually brimming with more tears, ready to fall.

AGE
Young and beautiful or old and haggard? Banshees take on both forms, but always bring the same sorrow.

VOICE
A banshee's wail is a sound you never want to hear. It combines the worst elements of a baby's cries, a wolf's call, and the mournful winds of death.

CLOTHING
Watch out for a woman in a long, gray cloak with a hood—she may be on the prowl for death. Some banshees wear death robes underneath their cloaks, while others wear a long, green dress.

Widely known as bearers of bad news, banshees are female fairies—but not in the pretty, dainty form known from childhood fairy tales. Instead, these spirits can be haggard and grim, and always mean that a human life is doomed. The appearance of a banshee is an omen of a death. A banshee traditionally "adopts" a family, and lets out an agonizing wail when one member is about to die. She begins to weep as if she will never stop crying. Sometimes she can be found washing the blood-stained clothes of the person, just before they pass away.

SIZE

▶ IT IS SAID THAT THE ANCIENT CELTIC PEOPLE, the Tuatha de Danann, were the fairy ancestors of the banshees. After defeat in a battle, they moved underground and lived in grassy mounds. Each group had a fairy heaven, known as "sidhe." The banshees leave these subterranean homes in search of their doomed, adoptive family. If several banshees appear at once, it foretells the death of somebody extremely important. A banshee can wail at the death of a family member even if he or she is far away, for example on a crusade or in battle.

WHERE IN THE WORLD?

The Celts spread across parts of Great Britain from central Europe. Most banshees attached themselves to Irish or Scottish families.

SCOTLAND

IRELAND
GREAT BRITAIN

DID YOU KNOW?

● Legend says that sprinkling oats on yourself, or keeping some in your pocket, can ward off banshees.

● The name "banshee" comes from the Irish "bean sidhe" meaning "woman of the fairy hill."

● Many Irish stories tell of the banshee singing to a dying ancestor to carry his or her soul across to the other world.

● A banshee's wail can be piercing enough to shatter glass, and should strike fear into the heart of anyone unlucky enough to hear it.

Black Annis

EYE
In most versions of the tale, Black Annis has only a single eye in the middle of her face.

STRENGTH
Don't be fooled by her old lady appearance: Black Annis is extremely strong and once she has you in her grip, there is no escape.

HANDS
The wizened crone has very long, strong fingers with claws instead of nails.

FACE
Black Annis is certainly noticeable, as she has wrinkled, blue skin and yellow fangs for teeth.

BODY
Annis is a shapeshifter, and can change her form into that of a black cat. She is sometimes called "Cat Anna."

This evil crone was said to live in Leicestershire, England, in a cave that she carved out of the stone herself, using only her clawed fingers to gouge away the rock. Outside the cave was an old oak tree that provided an excellent hiding place for Black Annis. She waited for passers-by, especially children, and then jumped out to catch them and drag them inside the cave. There, she skinned them alive and hung up the skins to dry. She feasted on the flesh and threw away the bones, but saved the dry skins to wear. If she became too hungry, she would resort to eating animals from local farms.

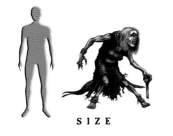

SIZE

▶ THREE CHILDREN WERE sent out one day to collect firewood. They gathered as much as they could, but night began to fall, and they became afraid that Black Annis would get them. Sure enough, they heard shuffling and snuffling, and turned to see her behind them. They dropped their firewood and ran back home, but she caught up with them at their cottage door. Their father hit her with an ax and she turned to run, but was struck down by the sound of the holy church bells that had begun to ring out for Christmas.

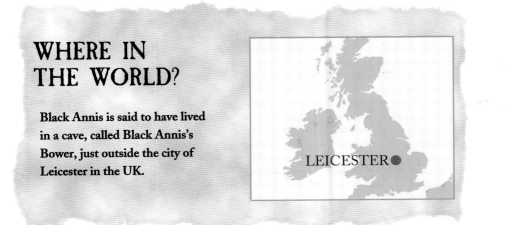

WHERE IN THE WORLD?

Black Annis is said to have lived in a cave, called Black Annis's Bower, just outside the city of Leicester in the UK.

LEICESTER ●

DID YOU KNOW?

● In Scotland, she is known as "Gentle Annie"; it was thought that flattering her with a nice name would make her look kindly on people and leave them alone.

● For many years, the people of Leicester staged a mock hunt to celebrate the end of winter. They dragged a dead cat, soaked in aniseed, to signify Black Annis.

● The cave can no longer be seen. With the passing of time, it gradually filled up with earth, and was covered over just after World War I to build houses.

● Annis's growls and teeth-grinding were so loud that the townsfolk were warned if she was coming, and could lock their doors and place herbs at the windows to prevent her from coming in.

Yuki-Onna

FACE
Her skin is ghostly pale, sometimes even see-through, but her eyes are terrifying and can freeze humans with fear.

BREATH
Yuki-Onna's breath is as cold as ice; she can freeze a human's body if she can keep them with her for long enough.

HAIR
Yuki-Onna's long, black hair flows in straight torrents down her back, and enhances her captivating image.

CLOTHES
She sometimes wears a beautiful Japanese kimono, as white as the snowy background so only her hair and face are visible.

This Japanese character appears during snowstorms, especially at night. She waits by the roadside and asks passers-by to help with her baby. If they accept, she freezes their body and sucks out their soul, or drains them of their blood. She is said to be a winter storm personified, both beautiful and life-threatening. Yuki-Onna sometimes visits mountain huts in search of vulnerable men. Her breath is powerful enough to blow down the doors of the huts. She bewitches the men and invites them outside into the cold, where she takes their souls as her prize.

SIZE

▶ ONE YOUNG MAN AND HIS FATHER were visited by the Yuki-Onna as they sheltered from a blizzard. The young man watched in horror as she leaned over his father and turned him to ice. She took a fancy to the young man and spared his life, but made him promise that he would never talk of what he had seen. Years later, sitting with his wife, he felt compelled to tell his story. His wife turned white and cold. "That Yuki-Onna was me and you have broken your promise," she hissed. She disappeared into the snow and was never seen again.

WHERE IN THE WORLD?

Tales of Yuki-Onna are told throughout Japan, but with variations in different parts of the country.

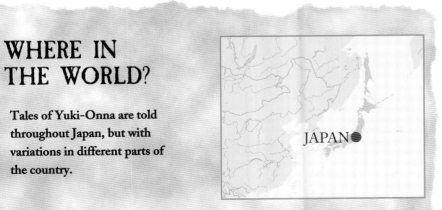

JAPAN ●

DID YOU KNOW?

• In Japanese, "yuki" means snow and "onna" means woman, making her the "snow woman."

• If anyone is brave enough to threaten or fight her, Yuki-Onna can evaporate into a puff of mist or fine snow to escape.

• In some versions of the tale, Yuki-Onna has blood-stained feet. In others, she leaves no footprints in the snow because of her ghostly form. Some even say she has no feet, which is common in Japanese ghost stories.

• Yuki-Onna may be the ghost of a woman who died in a snowstorm, although others say she was a princess of the Moon who came to Earth with a snowfall to look around, and then could not return to the sky.

Yama Uba

EYES
Despite her age, her eyes are piercing and full of life and vigor.

HAIR
She has extremely long, tangled white hair that she can bring to life to reel in her victims.

MOUTH
The old crone's mouth is said to be as wide as her face, stretching from ear to ear. In some tales, she has a second mouth at the top of her head.

CLOTHES
Her traditional red kimono may look beautiful from a distance, but up close it is dirty, ragged, and old.

Yama Uba is a ghost who takes the form of a frightening old woman lurking in the Japanese mountains. She seeks out people who are lost and invites them back to her home to help them. She offers food and drink, and a bed for the night—but then pounces on them as they sleep. She has an ax that she sharpens for every new victim, and is much feared by the inhabitants of the villages nearby. Yama Uba can turn herself into a beautiful young woman to make her victims feel safe, but many local people have seen her dancing at midnight in her real demonic form.

SIZE

▶ THIS EVIL SPIRIT HAS DIFFERENT methods of catching her victims. At times, instead of guiding them back to her mountain hut, she turns her hair into snakes. These lively creatures grab her prey and feed it into the mouth near the top of her head. Sometimes, pretending to help the poor lost travelers, she leads them along dangerous mountain paths until they are too weary to walk properly. When they totter and fall to their death, she climbs down and starts to feed on their flesh.

WHERE IN THE WORLD?

Yama Uba lurks in the forested areas in the mountains of Japan. Various regions tell tales of her wickedness and magic.

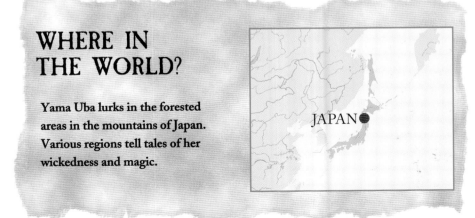

JAPAN ●

DID YOU KNOW?

● Her name means "Old woman in the mountains" from the Japanese "yama," which means mountain, and "uba," which means old woman or crone. Her name is also spelled Yamanba or Yamamba.

● Yama Uba is not fussy about who she eats. She usually captures adults who are traveling alone, but parents often warn their children about the dangers of straying too far from the house in case she whisks them away.

● In some Japanese tales Yama Uba raises a son, called Kintarou, who grows up to become a famous warrior and hero in national folklore.

● She is sometimes shown with mountain deer and monkeys alongside her.

Jikininki

SKIN
Jikininki have moldy, yellowish-gray skin. Their bodies are covered in scabs, wounds, and blisters.

HAIR
They are almost completely bald, but some still have random tufts of hair sticking out of their misshapen heads.

EYES
Their eyes glow red in their contorted faces, and they can kill or paralyze any unfortunate living person who looks them in the eye.

BODY
These ghoulish creatures are human in form, but hunched and decaying. They appear to be part-decomposed, with some muscles left on their thinning bodies.

ARMS
Strangely elongated arms end in deformed hands with clawlike fingers, which they use for digging bodies out of graves.

Jikininki are Japanese ghosts or undead, who feast on human corpses. They move around at night, raiding graveyards. In some tales, they can disguise themselves as normal human beings during the day. They are the spirits of people who lived greedy or selfish lives, and so are cursed to remain undead as punishment for their sins. Most of them are sound of mind and realize the horrors of what they do, and hate the constant hunger they have for human flesh. They cannot speak, but can grunt and squeal like wild animals. Many have jagged teeth for tearing at flesh and bones.

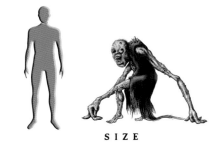

SIZE

▶ A PRIEST CALLED MUSO was witness to the horrible actions of a Jikininki. Being lost, he sought help from a village, where the people kindly gave him food and shelter. However, they said that a man had died that day and it was tradition that they must stay away from the village all night. Muso stayed behind, and was performing his priestly duties by the dead body when an evil spirit entered the room. Muso could not speak or move, but watched in horror as the dark shape lifted up the body and ate it, bones and all.

WHERE IN THE WORLD?

Jikininki are nomadic scavengers, constantly roaming the countryside to raid new graves. They are found mostly in Japan, but also in other parts of Asia.

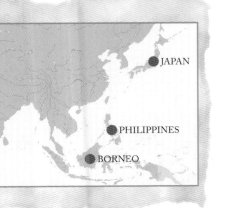

JAPAN

PHILIPPINES

BORNEO

DID YOU KNOW?

● Jikininki may steal from the bodies they eat, wearing their clothes and using any valuables they find to bribe important people to leave them alone.

● These greedy monsters hide behind tombstones or within shallow graves. They don't like to be seen, but if disturbed they will fight. Their claws and teeth are dangerous weapons, and any living person who is wounded by one may become infected with the Jikininki curse.

● The undead are hard to destroy. They cannot be poisoned or injured and they do not bleed.

● Jikininki are a form of "rakshasa," a Buddhist or Hindu demon. They can be put to rest with religious ceremonies called "segaki," which means "feeding the hungry ghosts."

Rokurokubi

NECK
A Rokurokubi's defining feature is its extremely long neck that can be stretched away from the body and act independently.

SPEECH
They can still speak normally when their head is stretched far from their body; some Rokurokubi hang out together at night.

HEAD
Even if separated from its body, the head can be identified as that of a Rokurokubi by a series of red characters at the base of the neck stump.

FACE
By day, the Rokurokubi's face is that of a normal person, but when it leaves its body behind it can transform into the frightening face of an ogre.

These creatures are one of the strangest-looking beings in Japanese folklore. By day, they live as normal humans, but at night they can stretch their necks like a garden hose to allow their heads to roam freely. Sometimes they are simply mischief-makers, frightening people who are out late at night. The more sinister ones among them prey on people, sucking their blood, and even eating them. A few don't know what's happening and remain asleep. Their only clue is strange dreams where they feel they are looking down on the world from a great height or a curious angle.

SIZE

▶ THERE IS A TALE OF AN EX-SAMURAI who becomes a priest and travels the length of his country. One night, he is invited to sleep in a hut. He gets up for a drink and is shocked to see five Rokurokubi bodies in the main room, each of them headless. Nevertheless, he is a brave man and takes action. He knows that the creatures can be killed by removing the body so its head cannot return. He watches one lost head as it bounces on the floor three times and then dies.

WHERE IN THE WORLD?

Watch out for Rokurokubi in all parts of Japan; they live in towns and cities as well as in quiet rural villages.

JAPAN●

DID YOU KNOW?

● Rokurokubi are a form of Japanese yokai, which means "bewitching apparition." They usually appear at dawn and dusk.

● Some of these creatures reveal themselves only to wicked or irreligious people. Others play it safe and let themselves be seen only by humans who will not be believed when they tell their tales, such as drunkards or simpletons.

● It is said that these monsters are created from people who do not follow the teachings of the Buddhist religion properly.

● It is possible for a Rokurokubi to live a normal life during the day and to get married and have children. Their husbands or wives only rarely find out, if they wake to find their partner's head high on a window ledge or door frame.

Adlet

TEETH
The adlet's teeth are dog-like, with extended canines and sharp incisors for biting and tearing flesh.

CHEST
An adlet's chest is big and muscly, and the heart of a wild animal beats inside. This creature can run constantly without getting tired.

FUR
With a red dog as their father, the adlet all have a reddish tinge to their fur.

HANDS
Although the hands are obviously related to human hands, with four fingers and a thumb, they are long and bony and have claws instead of nails.

LIMBS
More human in form than a dog, an adlet has long, well-developed legs that are obviously different from its forearms. It walks on two legs like a human.

The adlet is part-human and part-canine, with a fearsome beast of a dog as a father. Initially there were just five of them, but they bred and produced more of their race. An adlet is bloodthirsty, and prey on both humans and animals. They can even be cannibals, eating other dogs. When they first hunt down their prey they go for the victim's throat and drink the fresh blood. Mostly, they continue to eat the flesh and insides of their victim. If possible, they hunt together to make it easier to trap their prey.

SIZE

► THE STORY GOES THAT AN INUIT WOMAN married a giant red dog and became pregnant with his children. She was obviously forced out of society for this unnatural act. Ten children were born covered with fur, and closely resembled puppies as much as human babies. The terrified woman sent five of them on a boat to Europe, where they formed the basis of the "white races," as the Inuit called them. The remaining five grew to be the ferocious creatures known as adlet.

WHERE IN THE WORLD?

The Inuit people who tell tales of the adlet live in the remote north, in the USA, Canada, and nearby islands.

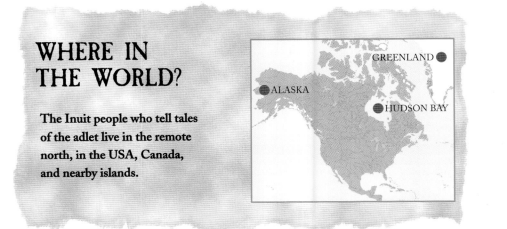

GREENLAND

ALASKA

HUDSON BAY

DID YOU KNOW?

● The adlet are part of Inuit folklore, and their story is known in and around the Arctic Circle, including Alaska, the east Canadian coast, and Greenland.

● In Greenland and Baffin Island (off the east coast of Canada), the creatures are known by the name erqigdlit. They are said to be the offspring of the original adlet.

● The tales sometimes treat the erqigdlit as literally half-human, half-dog, with the body and face of a person and rear legs of a canine. If they see a human they will give chase and make sure they catch and kill to get their fill of meat.

● Some stories suggest that the adlet's mother married a werewolf, rather than an actual dog.

Nidhogg

HEIGHT
According to some sources, Nidhogg is taller than a multi-story building. It can rear up on its hind legs but walks on all fours.

JAWS
Nidhogg's teeth are sharp and housed in powerful jaws. They ooze with the juice from corpses and tree-root sap.

WINGS
The dragon can fly with its enormous wings. Its five fingerlike bones are spanned by leathery skin to allow it to take to the air.

SCALES
Most of Nidhogg's body is covered with impressive body armor. It also has spikes on its back, tail, neck, and head, and a full set of killer claws.

Nidhogg is a mighty dragon from Norse and Germanic legend. It lives in the realm of the dead known as Niflheim or Helheim, and its name means "the tearer of corpses." Nidhogg eats the flesh of dead people, thrown down to it from Earth. It is also known to suck the blood of life's less honorable characters, such as liars, cheats, and murderers. Niflheim is a fitting home for these abominable people: it is the darkest, coldest, and lowest of the nine worlds of the dead. Nidhogg's home is a pit of venomous serpents near Hvergelmir, or "the bubbling cauldron," a spring that is the source of the world's rivers.

SIZE

▶ AS A CHANGE FROM EATING DEAD FLESH and drinking blood, Nidhogg sometimes chews at the roots of Yggdrasil, the tree of life. It finally succeeds in gnawing through the roots of the tree, with the help of four serpents, but this sparks a war on Earth. After a dreadful three-year winter, the gods fight the frost giants in a monumental battle at Ragnarok. Nidhogg is involved but is not killed. Instead, the dragon survives and returns to its home, where it feasts on the many bodies thrown to it from the battlefield.

WHERE IN THE WORLD?

Tales of Nidhogg encompass myths from many northern European countries, including Germany, Denmark, Sweden, Norway, Iceland, and the Netherlands.

ICELAND
SWEDEN
NORWAY
DENMARK
GERMANY

DID YOU KNOW?

● An eagle lives at the top of the tree of life. Nidhogg sometimes breaks from its meal of corpses to send a squirrel up the tree to torment the eagle.

● Nidhogg's name is sometimes said to mean "the dread biter," "striking full of hatred," or "evil blow."

● Some stories say that when Nidhogg entered the battle of Ragnarok, it took corpses with it to help with the fighting.

● A dragon or monster named Nidhogg appears as a character in several computer and video games, and also in a Viking Lego® set.

Yara-ma-yha-who

HEIGHT
He is small and deformed, able to sit unseen in fig trees and prey upon unsuspecting travelers.

DIGITS
The tips of his fingers and toes are covered with suckers, like those of an octopus. He uses them to hold his prey in place and suck their blood.

HEAD
For his overall size, the yara-ma-yha-who has an enormous head and a huge mouth. He has no teeth but swallows his food whole.

SKIN
The yara-ma-yha-who is not a pretty sight. For starters, he is bright red, the color of his victims' blood.

How do you eat people if you have no teeth? If you're the yara-ma-yha-who from Australian aboriginal mythology, you swallow them whole! This evil creature lives in fig trees, where he waits for passers-by to rest in the shade. He jumps on them, pins them down, and sucks out their blood. The weakened victim is left alive, and the yara-ma-yha-who goes wandering to work up a real appetite. Upon his return, he gulps the victim like a snake swallowing its prey. Then, the creature stands up and dances to shake its food down to its stomach.

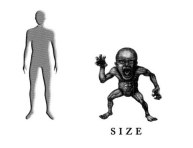

SIZE

▶ BEING EATEN BY THE YARA-MA-YHA-WHO doesn't result in death. Instead, his victims are regurgitated after the yara-ma-yha-who has quenched his thirst with water and slept off his food coma. The victim is reborn, but is slightly shorter than before they were consumed. Several people have been caught more than once, getting shorter and redder each time they are brought back up. Eventually, the process is just too much, and the victim emerges as a wizened, red-skinned, vampiric creature—another yara-ma-yha-who has been created.

WHERE IN THE WORLD?

This wicked little vampire occupies many territories across Australia.

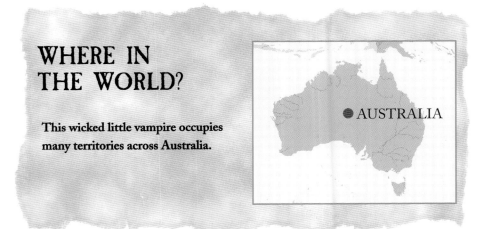

● AUSTRALIA

DID YOU KNOW?

● Usually, a victim can survive three attacks before he is turned into a yara-ma-yha-who himself.

● The best way to elude this vampire is to play dead. When he returns from his walk, pretend to be a corpse. He will tickle you and poke you with a stick to test whether you are truly lifeless.

● If you pass the tickle test, the yara-ma-yha-who will sit and watch from a distance, looking for any signs of life. He may fall asleep, giving you the chance to escape.

● Those who are lucky enough to reach this stage stand a strong chance of survival. The vampire's strange legs are not built for sprinting; in fact, he runs like a wobbling bird.

Impundulu

BEAK
The impundulu's beak is vivid scarlet—the color of blood.

FEATHERS
The bird's feathers are pure white, in contrast to its legs and beak. Other accounts describe it as having a body covered in a rainbow of colored feathers.

LEGS
The huge talons enable Impundulu to hold down victims while feeding on them.

WINGS
Watch out for the wings! They can shoot out bolts of electricity, like lightning, from their feathered ends.

This bird is the size of a man, with mighty wings that produce lightning from the tips. It can create thunder with a flap of these wings, and it's said that forked lightning is the bird's droppings falling from on high. The impundulu feeds on human blood, holding onto its victims with its fearsome talons. It has an almost unquenchable thirst. The birds are kept as servants, or

SIZE

familiars, by witches and witch doctors, and sent out to attack their enemies. The creatures are also used to spread disease and infection. A faithful familiar will be handed down through a family of witches.

▶ YOUNG WOMEN ARE THE favorite victim of the impundulu. In order to capture them, the bird takes on the form of an attractive young man, who charms the young women until they are easy prey. If he is successful, the woman may become his slave or even be turned into a witch. The men are recognizable through their disguise by "witch sniffers," who are able to detect a witch or a witch's familiar whatever form.

WHERE IN THE WORLD?

Tales of the impundulu are told across South Africa by tribes such as the Zulu, Pondo, and Xhosa.

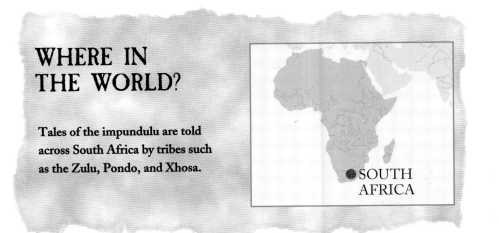

● SOUTH AFRICA

DID YOU KNOW?

● This bird is almost impossible to destroy. If you catch it, it should be burned to death to prevent it from coming back to life.

● Some local healers possess a special magical cream or lotion made from impundulu fat, which protects its wearers from an attack by the creature.

● The impundulu is linked to illnesses that involve bleeding, such as hemorrhage and miscarriage.

● The bird's name translates as "lightning bird." It uses owls and eagles, which are seen as evil omens of death, as its servants.

● Said to be the most evil of a witch's familiars, the impundulu has strong magic. If it sees blood, it becomes frenzied and will attack any humans nearby.

Boo Hag

HAIR
The hag's flowing locks are long and as red as her body. Her hair stands on end, though, so it won't tickle and wake her sleeping victim.

EYES
It's unlikely you will ever look a boo hag in the eye—her victims are deep in slumber, after all. If you did wake, though, you would see hollow black pits where her eyes should be.

SKIN
Strictly speaking, a boo hag has no skin of her own. She is bright red in appearance, because her muscles are on the outside. This makes her warm to the touch, like raw meat.

MOUTH
The gaping hollow in a boo hag's face is a horror-filled hole used to suck the breath from her victims.

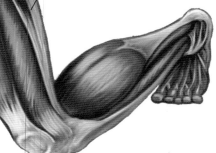

Like vampires, boo hags roam in the night, looking for victims to feed on. However, the boo hag doesn't suck blood. She steals a person's breath by sucking it out of them while they sleep. This is known as "ridin,'" and you might hear the warning "Don't let de hag ride ya" in areas where she hunts. The hag flies to her victim's house and enters through a crack or hole, such as a keyhole. As she sucks the breath, her prey sleeps soundly and dreamlessly. They won't know they've been ridden, although they will feel tired the next morning.

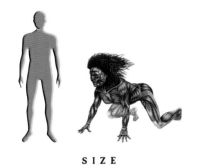

SIZE

▶ BOO HAGS ARE INFAMOUS FOR stealing human skin to disguise themselves. If a victim struggles and tries to wake, the boo hag will abandon the breath-sucking and strip the skin off their prey's body. Wearing it like baby's clothes, she can roam freely and choose her next victim. Before going ridin', she undresses from the skin and hides it for when she returns. There's one small catch, though. The boo hag must be back in the skin before dawn, or she will be trapped without skin forever.

WHERE IN THE WORLD?

The boo hag goes "ridin'" in the southern state of South Carolina in the USA.

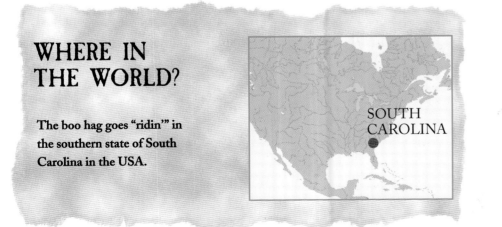

SOUTH CAROLINA

DID YOU KNOW?

● To stay safe, it's said you should sleep with a broom by your bedside. The hags are distracted by counting the straws in the broom, and run out of time to conduct their gruesome business.

● The boo hag is a Gullah legend, told by the African American communities of South Carolina. The Gullah language and culture still retain much from their African roots.

● A boo hag usually steals her victim's skin who struggles and tries to wake while being ridden.

● In one tale, the boo hags marry unsuspecting men and deliver them to the "boo daddy," who eats their flesh. To get rid of the hag, her husband must fill her empty skin with salt and pepper, which will burn her raw muscled body.

Loogaroo

FACE
Even without a covering of skin, her face shows her age. Her features are shrunken and withered.

SKIN
As part of her transformation into a vampire, a loogaroo must take off her skin to reveal her bones and muscles inside.

GLOW
In readiness for her night travels, the loogaroo has a faint glow of light around her skinless body.

HABITS
Like many other types of vampire, the loogaroo is obsessive. She can be stopped from entering a house by sprinkling sand in front of the doorway. She should take so long counting the grains that daylight comes before she can attack.

In Haiti and other islands of the West Indies, a loogaroo is an old woman who has made a deal with the devil in return for magical powers. The problem is, to keep her side of the deal, she has to supply the devil with fresh blood every night. It can come from animals or humans, but if she fails to feed her diabolical business partner, he will take some of her blood instead— which will eventually kill her. It is said that these women can shape-shift into an animal form. Quite often this is a goat, a creature with unfortunate associations with the devil.

SIZE

▶ As NIGHT FALLS, hunting time begins for the loogaroo. First, she proceeds to her local "Devil tree"—a type of silk-cotton tree, or Jumbie tree, found in the West Indies. There, she removes her skin, folds it up very carefully, and hides it by turning it into a ball of sulfurous fire. Then, she travels through the darkness as a flickering blob of light, like a will-o'-the-wisp. She can enter her victim's house through any crack, where she sucks up the blood she needs to keep her pact with the devil.

WHERE IN THE WORLD?

The loogaroo is talked about in many Caribbean countries, including Haiti and Grenada, and in the southern US state of Louisiana.

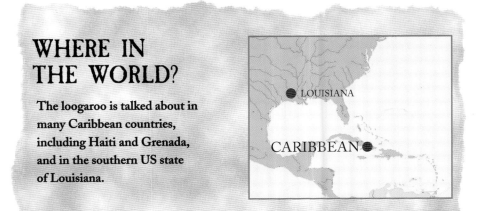

LOUISIANA

CARIBBEAN

DID YOU KNOW?

● If the loogaroo is injured while in her animal form, the wound will show when she regains her human body.

● Check out the shadow of any suspected loogaroo—she may well cast a shadow in the shape of an animal.

● The loogaroo's victims feel exhausted and—literally—drained the next day.

● Many people believe that they have seen the loogaroo's light flashing through the darkness. Some say that the loogaroo's skin can be retrieved and mashed in a mortar with salt and pepper to kill off the vampire.

● These creatures are hateful to dogs, which will bark madly at them. If a person is constantly attacked by dogs, he or she may be a shapeshifter.

Lobisomem

HEIGHT
Although transformed from humans, many lobisomem are extremely tall when they rear up on their hind legs.

BODY
A lobisomem's body is completely covered in fur. Quite often it is pale gray in color, making it glow spookily in the light of the moon.

FACE
When fully transformed, a lobisomem's face is totally wolf-like, with an extended muzzle containing long, pointed teeth. Its eyes may glow red or yellow when it hunts.

LEGS
Unlike some types of werewolf, these creatures hunt on four legs, prowling across country and pouncing on all fours. They have paws instead of feet and hands.

The world is full of tales of werewolves: afflicted humans who are cursed to change into wolflike creatures under the influence of a full moon. This condition is called lycanthropy, from the Ancient Greek words for "wolf-human." Lobisomem are the werewolves of Portuguese and Brazilian folklore: their name comes from the Portuguese word "lobo," which means wolf. They are often said to be tortured by their own condition, feeling distraught at what happens when they change. By the light of a full Moon they become vicious, strong carnivores, either capturing live victims who are out alone, or digging up bodies from new graves to eat them.

SIZE

► THE EASIEST WAY TO BECOME a werewolf is to fall prey to another werewolf's attack. A single bite will cause the victim to become infected. Many lobisomem attacks are frenzied and vicious enough to kill a person, which is a merciful release from a lifetime of misery every full Moon. It is said that any person with eyebrows that meet in the middle, claw-like fingernails, or an unusually long third finger is a werewolf. Many South American tales say that the seventh son in a family will be cursed to change into a werewolf.

WHERE IN THE WORLD?

Lobisomem are native to Portuguese-speaking people, in the European country itself and in its former colony Brazil.

PORTUGAL

BRAZIL

DID YOU KNOW?

● To tell if a creature is a real wolf or a cursed werewolf, it has no tail, like many supernatural creatures that assume a real-world form.

● Modern tales say that lobisomem can be killed by a silver bullet, but the original folktales were around long before guns with metal bullets were invented.

● If a werewolf is killed with a silver object through the heart, it will return to its human form.

● If you can catch a werewolf, you may be able to cure it. Hurting its paws will change it back into its human form. It will have wounds on its hands and feet which must be kept open with hot candle wax. If they are dressed like this for three Sundays, the werewolf will be driven out.

The Beast of Bray Road

BODY
The beast is described as having a large, heavy body and powerful chest, like that of a person who works out in the gym.

LIMBS
The beast has been seen walking and crouching on all fours, but attacks on two legs like a running person. It holds its food between its front paws to eat, much like a bear.

HEAD
Like a wild animal, the beast has a snout, pointed ears, and large fangs. Its eyes glow yellow, like an animal caught in the headlights.

FUR
Whether it is a wolflike, doglike, or bearlike creature, it is always said to have gray-brown hair all over its body.

Is the Beast of Bray Road an actual werewolf? It depends on what, and who, you believe. In the 1980s and 1990s there were many sightings of this creature, skulking in the undergrowth and looking for meat to eat. Most people described it as a large, strong, heavy, and hairy creature. They don't always agree on what kind of animal it most resembled. One thing is for sure, though—the beast doesn't eat people. Moviemakers have turned the beast into a more sinister creature that terrorizes humans and eats them, but in real life it seems that it would rather run away than attack a human.

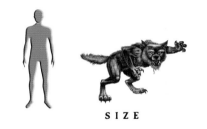

SIZE

▶ ONE MAN WHO SAW THE BEAST was working at night, collecting roadkill to keep the highways clear. He was sitting at the roadside in his truck, filling out paperwork, when the truck began to shake. In his mirror, he could see a large, furry beast. It was standing on two legs and helping itself to a deer from the back of the truck. The Beast had found a ready meal for supper! The man quickly drove off, frightened, and when he returned only five minutes later, both creature and deer had disappeared.

WHERE IN THE WORLD?

Bray Road is a two-mile stretch of road through Wisconsin farmland, but the Beast has been seen in many areas in the southeast of the state.

WISCONSIN ●

DID YOU KNOW?

● Cryptozoologists (scientists in search of new creatures and proof that they exist) think that the Beast might be some kind of Bigfoot.

● The Beast is reported as being 7 feet (2.1 m) tall and weighing maybe 200 pounds (91 kg).

● A journalist, named Linda Godfrey has spent many years researching sightings of the creature. She says that a large number of the sightings are reported near sacred Native American sites such as burial grounds.

● Strange happenings in the area—mutilated animal bodies and unusual lights in the night sky—have led some people to believe in an occult or supernatural link to the creature. They think it could certainly be a shapeshifter like a werewolf.

The Wolf Man

CLOTHES
During his transformation into the Wolf Man, Larry Talbot's clothes remain in place, although they are too small for his muscle-bound animal body.

FOREHEAD
As he changes into the Wolf Man, Larry's forehead becomes grotesquely deformed and enlarged.

HANDS
The Wolf Man has paws for hands, with five claws and pointed nails.

FACE
Wolflike features transform Larry's nose and mouth, with its terrible extended canine teeth, and his face is covered in fur. He does not develop the muzzle and ears of a wolf, though.

FEET
Like giant paws, the Wolf Man's hairy feet have only four toes to walk on. Each of these toes has a large claw.

Not just any old werewolf, the main character in this movie from 1941 is literally part-wolf and still part-man. Whereas other werewolves make a complete transformation under a full moon, the Wolf Man remains vaguely human in appearance. He walks on two legs, and his face is still recognizable as that of a person (although he is, admittedly, a very, VERY hairy person).

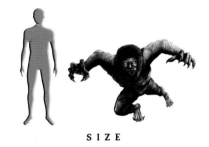

SIZE

While still human, he hears an old poem that will stay with him: "Even a man who is pure in heart and says his prayers by night, May become a wolf when the wolfsbane blooms and the autumn moon is bright."

▶ A NEWCOMER TO WALES, Larry Talbot knows little of werewolves until he buys an antique walking stick decorated with a silver wolf's head. He is told that it represents a werewolf, and hears the poem for the first time. That night, while trying to rescue a friend from a wolf attack, he is bitten—and is turned into a werewolf himself. He is doomed to prowl at night in search of prey. The Wolf Man is finally defeated by his father, who kills him with his own silver-headed walking stick.

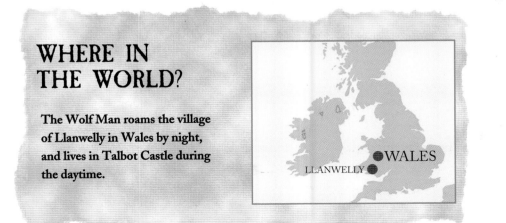

WHERE IN THE WORLD?

The Wolf Man roams the village of Llanwelly in Wales by night, and lives in Talbot Castle during the daytime.

WALES

LLANWELLY

DID YOU KNOW?

- Unlike many werewolves, the Wolf Man is not transformed by the light of the full Moon, but only when the wolfsbane blooms in the fall.

- Wolfsbane is a flower said to have supernatural powers. It can turn an infected person into a werewolf if they smell, wear, or eat the plant.

- The Wolf Man appears in several movies after the original 1941 black and white movie. These later movies often change his characteristics, such as the times when he is able to transform.

- Not all werewolves are vulnerable to silver. Usually, this is more associated with vampires.

- The werewolf who bites Larry is a gypsy called Bela, a fortune-teller's son. He has suffered the curse of lycanthropy (being a werewolf) for years.

Nosferatu

EYES
With vivid black rings around the edges, Count Orlok's eyes are wild and disturbing. His bushy eyebrows make him look even more threatening.

FINGERS
Long, bony fingers that end in claw-like, pointed nails make the nosferatu a real creature of horror—especially if he is creeping up on his next victim with fingers outstretched.

HEAD
The Count has strangely pointed ears and very little hair. His smile reveals the pointed fangs of a true vampire.

BODY
Nosferatu never eat food, surviving only on their diet of blood. This makes them slender. Their habit of sleeping in coffins gives them a stiff, upright stance.

Nosferatu is the title of a classic vampire movie, and is another word for vampire. The main character is Count Orlok, who drinks the blood of human victims. He is so thirsty that he even tries to suck the wounded finger of one of his guests. The guest is an estate agent visiting the Count's castle in Transylvania. The Count leaves his home in Transylvania to live in Germany, across the road from the agent and his wife. If a nosferatu is caught in sunlight, he bursts into a puff of fire and smoke. This is how Count Orlok is eventually trapped by the wife, although it costs her her own life.

SIZE

▶ COUNT ORLOK TRAVELS BY SHIP, in a soil-filled coffin. By the time the ship arrives in Germany, the crew are all dead, with suspicious puncture marks on their bodies. The ship is full of rats that are thought to have brought the plague to Orlok's new hometown. The estate agent's wife, in possession of a book on vampires, reads that nosferatu can also spread the plague. The only way to rid her town of its sickness and sorrow is to offer herself to Count Orlok. She tricks him into staying too long, so that he is trapped by the rising Sun in her window.

WHERE IN THE WORLD?

Count Orlok moves from his castle in Transylvania to the town of Wisborg in northern Germany, where he preys upon the townsfolk.

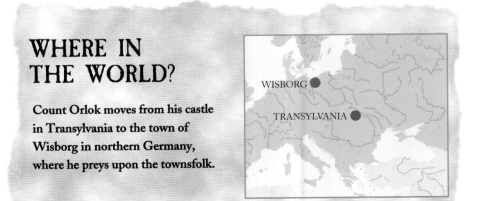

WISBORG

TRANSYLVANIA

DID YOU KNOW?

● Count Orlok carries soil in his coffin, as nosferatu get their power from the soil they were buried in.

● It is probable that the estate agent becomes transformed into a new nosferatu by Count Orlok.

● The original movie version of *Nosferatu* was made in 1922 and starred Max Schreck as the Count. The movie was made using the basic story of Bram Stoker's *Dracula*, but with new names and ideas.

● Unlike Count Dracula, whose victims usually become new vampires, Count Orlok's victims most often die from the plague.

● The original movie is a silent movie in black-and-white. The story is told through words on the screen and music increases the drama.

Christopher Lee as Dracula

HAIR
Dracula's hair is swept back
from his forehead to reveal
his bristling eyebrows, and
forms a characteristic
M-shaped hairline.

FACE
He has well-defined
features with
pronounced
cheekbones, a strong
nose, and dark,
hollow eyes—which
all add up to a
frightening but
classic image.

VOICE
Cold and hard enough to
send shivers down your
spine, his voice is deep and
menacing with an impeccable
English accent.

HEIGHT
One of the tallest of all
famous actors, at 6 feet
5 inches (195.6 cm),
Christopher Lee towers
over his victims.

ozens of movies have been made about Count Dracula. Many people have their own idea of what the Count looks like, and their imagination may well conjure up a picture of Christopher Lee, the actor who played Dracula in a Hammer Horror movie from 1958. He is remembered for playing an evil but human character who seeks revenge for wrongs done against him, and feels fear when he is facing death. He swooshes around in his long black cape and looks extremely aristocratic and imposing, although he doesn't speak much.

SIZE

► THE FIRST TIME CHRISTOPHER LEE bared his fangs as Dracula, he faced Peter Cushing, another famous actor, playing the vampire hunter Dr. Van Helsing. Their characters meet in the movie's finale. As dawn approaches, Van Helsing comes face-to-face with the Count. Dramatically, he runs across a table as they battle with each other, tearing down a drape as he leaps, exposing Dracula to the daylight. Holding two candlesticks together as a cross, Van Helsing forces Dracula into the searing sunshine, where he disintegrates into dust.

WHERE IN THE WORLD?

In the movie, the Count lives in Transylvania but is followed to Karlstadt in Germany, where he has chosen Lucy as his victim.

KARLSTADT
TRANSYLVANIA ●

DID YOU KNOW?

● In 2004 *Total Film* magazine listed *Dracula* as the 30th greatest British movie of all time.

● The movie was called *Dracula* in most countries except the USA, where it was titled *Horror of Dracula* to avoid it being confused with the 1931 *Dracula* starring Bela Lugosi as the Count.

● Christopher Lee was so popular in the part that he starred as Dracula in seven more movies for Hammer Studios.

● The 1958 movie reinforced the idea from folklore that vampires can be burned by a crucifix and that they are mortally afraid of sunshine.

Zombie (from *I Walked with a Zombie*)

EYES
Jessica's eyes are open but unseeing. They are glazed and unfocused, staring only into the distance.

HAIR
Her blonde hair is part of what makes Jessica so attractive to both of the brothers, turning them into rivals.

FACE
Although she has lost any spark of life or personality, Jessica is still the beautiful woman she always was.

WALKING
Jessica walks around in a trance, with her arms stretched out in front, but without the strange stiff limbs and wobbling walk of other kinds of zombies.

Jessica Holland sleepwalks every night, and her doctor has diagnosed an incurable tropical fever as the cause. This affects her spinal cord and brain, and makes her unable to speak. Locals say her illness has made her mindless. But her nurse, Betsy, finds out the truth: Jessica is a zombie. Unlike zombies of other movies, raised from the dead, Jessica is a Voodoo-created zombie. If her flesh is cut, she does not bleed. She doesn't grow old. She is undead as a punishment for her love for two half-brothers.

SIZE

▶ TO TRY TO CURE JESSICA, Betsy calls on the help of the local Voodoo priest. She is shocked when she is summoned into the priest's hut and finds out it is a white doctor of medicine, Mrs. Rand. She says that Jessica can never be cured, but outside the hut the natives are practicing their own rituals on Jessica. They test her with a sword and decide that she is a bloodless zombie: a member of the living dead. She has been cursed by none other than Mrs. Rand, possessed by a Voodoo god!

WHERE IN THE WORLD?

The Hollands and their nurse, Betsy Connell, live on a sugar plantation on the mythical Caribbean island of San Sebastian.

SAN SEBASTIAN

DID YOU KNOW?

● The worshippers meet at a "houmfort," which is a Voodoo temple. Voodoo is an Afro-American religion practiced in the southern United States and parts of the Caribbean, especially Haiti.

● Many people on the island are descended from slaves who were brought on a boat with a figurehead called "Ti-Misery." This figurehead is now a statue on the island, and forms part of the Voodoo religion.

● San Sebastian is such a sad place for the old slave families that they still cry when a new baby is born, and rejoice at a funeral.

● Betsy's character is based on Charlotte Brontë's famous heroine, Jane Eyre, who falls in love with her cold-hearted employer in his grand but joyless home.

Zombies (from *Night of the Living Dead*)

MOUTH
They have bad teeth with obvious rotten areas and blood around the lips.

BRAIN
Although they are dead, these zombies are still capable of some thought—such as how to attack their victims. They cannot speak but can make moaning noises.

EYES
All of the zombies appear to be in a walking trance, like sleepwalkers, with open, staring, hollow eyes.

SKIN
Zombies are noted for their pale complexion and bad skin.

BODY
After death, the body stiffens. Their stiff legs and arms give them their recognizable lurching walk.

The zombies from the movie *Night of the Living Dead* are a virtual army of assassins, on the hunt for flesh and blood. At first glance, they may look like ordinary people, but their stiff, lumbering walk and staring eyes reveal their true identity. Scientists in the story suggest that they have been affected by radiation from an exploded Venus space probe. The zombies are newly-dead people who get up and walk again. Most have come from mortuaries and cemeteries before they are buried. They are extremely strong, and their grasping hands can break through blockades to grab their victims.

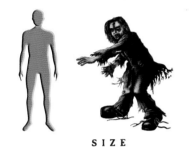

SIZE

▶ BARBARA AND BEN (someone she meets) think they are the only ones hiding from the zombies in a remote country house, until they meet five more people sheltering in the cellar. Together, they try to scare off the creatures with fire bombs and flaming torches, but hordes of zombies circle the house. In the cellar, one young girl recovers from her injuries and reveals herself as one of the ghoulish creatures, and begins to attack her family and feast on the flesh of the people trapped there with her.

WHERE IN THE WORLD?

The characters hide in a Pennsylvania farmhouse, but see on the TV news that the zombies are roaming throughout the entire eastern seaboard of the USA.

PENNSYLVANIA

EASTERN SEABOARD

DID YOU KNOW?

● Barbara and her brother, Johnny, are first attacked in a graveyard by a single zombie. Johnny is injured, and later comes back as a zombie to attack the hostages in the house.

● Inside the house, Ben and Barbara find the remains of a dead woman who has been partially devoured by the zombies.

● The only way to kill these creatures is to shoot or injure them in the head. Their brain has been reactivated by the radiation, so it is their weak spot and must be destroyed. If you manage to kill one, it should be soaked with gasoline and burned immediately before it comes back to "life" once again.

● Zombies are slow and lumbering and, if you keep your wits about you, you can outrun one. They are also afraid of fire.

Index